Educating for Global Citizenship

A practical guide for schools

Boyd Roberts

International® Baccalaureate

Educating for Global Citizenship

Published March 2009

International Baccalaureate
Peterson House, Malthouse Avenue, Cardiff Gate
Cardiff, Wales GB CF23 8GL
United Kingdom
Phone: +44 29 2054 7777
Fax: +44 29 2054 7778
Website: http://www.ibo.org

The International Baccalaureate (IB) offers three high quality and challenging
educational programmes for a worldwide community of schools, aiming to
create a better, more peaceful world.

IB merchandise and publications can be purchased through the IB store at
http://store.ibo.org. General ordering queries should be directed to the sales
and marketing department in Cardiff.
Phone: +44 29 2054 7746
Fax: +44 29 2054 7779
Email: sales@ibo.org

British Library Cataloguing in Publication Data.
A catalogue record for this book is available from the British Library.
ISBN: 978-1-906345-16-7

Cover design by Pentacorbig, High Wycombe, UK
Typeset and illustrated by Prepress Projects Ltd, Perth, UK
Printed and bound by Athenaeum Press, Gateshead, UK

Item code GD193

2009 2010 2011 2012 2013
10 9 8 7 6 5 4 3 2 1

Acknowledgments

We are grateful for permission to reprint the following copyright texts: Extracts from an
article in is magazine (Volume 10, issue 1, Autumn 2007) reproduced with the permission
of the Editor and Publishers, John Catt Educational Ltd.

The material on page 110 is adapted by the publisher from "Education for Global
Citizenship: A Guide for Schools" Oxfam Publishing, 1 March 2006, with the permission
of Oxfam GB, Oxfam House, John Smith Drive, Cowley, Oxford OX4 2JY UK www.oxfam.
org.uk. Oxfam GB does not necessarily endorse any text or activities that accompany the
materials, nor has it approved the adapted text.

To my parents, Kath and Frank, for laying the foundations for global citizenship

To Jackie, for continuing love and support

To Karson and his generation, who will be taking over

Activities

Annual income vs. world's population (4)

CONTENTS

Introduction

For simplicity, this book is called *Educating for Global Citizenship*. Educating *for* indicates the purpose, direction and outcome towards which education is focused. A key principle running through the book is that students are global citizens now. So, the book is equally concerned with education *in* global citizenship. It is also concerned with education *about* global issues. But it is not concerned with education *about* global citizenship. Within these pages we are concerned with how global citizenship is practised, not how it is studied.

There are some excellent initiatives in global citizenship education and related areas in many parts of the world, and doubtless many more in languages I cannot access. Most materials for schools relate to one national context only. This book attempts to bring together selected research and practice from a number of countries, and is addressed to an international readership of teachers and school administrators. Therefore, you will need to relate it to your own specific context. While working through this book, and subsequently, you may find it helpful to keep a journal, recording your own thoughts and developing understanding of (educating for) global citizenship and how it relates to your life and work. Some activities in the book call for written responses, and looking back on these later may be interesting.

People picking up the book are in very different places—in terms of location, context and perspective—and will be looking for different things. You should, of course, do as you will with the book. But it is structured to provide a map for a journey, as you explore—individually, or perhaps with colleagues—some of the context and implications of educating young people for a good life in a global world. So, the first few chapters provide background, raise issues, probe thinking and set the scene before plunging into practicalities. (Although the theoretical literature is extensive, it is only briefly touched on here, to give space for more practical issues.) I hope the journey will prove interesting, wherever your starting point. Fast-forward if you will, but jump about and you may lose your way!

The book is a map, not a route. Key questions, reflections and activities are an integral part of the book and will contribute to your unfolding perspective and sense of direction. Case studies illustrate how schools on their journeys are already responding to global dimensions and challenges and working to develop global citizens.

While personal understanding is necessary, discussing and sharing ideas with others seems particularly appropriate—perhaps essential—when considering this area. Global citizenship education benefits enormously from a coordinated school approach involving the whole community. I hope the book may help in this.

I am very grateful to all colleagues who have helped shape my thinking and practice over the years in international education and, latterly, global citizenship education. In direct connection with this book, thanks are due to those who have responded to inquiries, and, particularly, to those from many countries who have provided the written contributions that are an important feature of the book.

Many thanks also to Malcolm McKenzie and George Walker for helpful suggestions in the early stages, to Keith Allen, Sheila Burch, Mary Hayden and Kwok Cheung Law, who have commented on drafts of sections of the book. I am particularly grateful to Clayton Lewis and Harriet Marshall, who read the entire manuscript, and made detailed, helpful comments. It is also a pleasure to acknowledge the contribution of Sophie Matta, Vicky McHale and Katya Vines of the IB publications group, and Susannah Fountain, for their encouragement and input in getting from ideas to print.

Unless our global citizenship initiatives in schools produce beneficial changes in students, they are worthless. This book similarly is only worthwhile if it has some impact on thinking and practice, however modest.

1 Living and learning in a global world

Although trade and migration have gone on for thousands of years, the scale and scope of our connections today are unprecedented. Economically, companies have global spread and foreign governments own major stakes in key operations in other countries. Credit lending in the United States (USA) precipitates economic shockwaves around the world. The extent of our interconnections has given rise to a new language to describe them. "Global" was coined in the nineteenth century, and the word "globalization" in the 1940s. "Globalization" has itself been globalized, through the new global language of English, and has found its way into all major languages.

Scholte (2002: 5) draws a parallel with earlier times:

> *"When Jeremy Bentham coined the word 'international' in the 1780s, the concept caught hold because it resonated of a growing trend of his day, namely, the rise of nation-states and cross-border transactions between them. The current proliferation of global talk also seems unlikely to be accidental. The popularity of the terminology arguably reflects a widespread intuition that contemporary social relations have acquired an important new character."*

Our new words reflect a new reality. For our purposes, we can consider globalization to be "a widening, deepening and speeding up of interconnectedness in all aspects of contemporary social life from the cultural to the criminal, the financial to the spiritual" (Held et al 1999: 2).

Environmentally too, we are interconnected. Activities in one place affect water and air quality in countries miles away; even the climate of the whole planet. And while the human population grows, our "ecological footprint" increases and biodiversity and populations of other species decline (WWF 2008).

In the 1960s, Marshall McLuhan introduced the phrase "global village", which swept the world, demonstrating its validity (Symes 1995). A name was needed for the inhabitants of the global village, and the "global citizen" emerged. New connections, new words and a new way of seeing ourselves. We can even pinpoint our position in the global village—at least in crude financial terms.

Activity

Visit http://www.globalrichlist.com, to insert your annual income and see where it places you in relation to the world's population. Try also inserting the pocket money, or the examination fees, for one student taking public examinations in your school.

This simple exercise raises questions about the lives and welfare of some of our global village neighbours, while demonstrating the power of another global phenomenon—global communications. Images and information come streaming into our computers and on to our mobile phones. Rainforests being felled, polar icecaps melting, events and disasters across the globe—9/11, earthquakes, the Beijing Olympics—brought directly to us through vivid images that lodge indelibly in our minds. McLuhan (1964: 4) noted: "In the electric age ... we necessarily participate ... in the consequences of our every action." We have the communications. We get the information. And with knowledge comes responsibility.

All of our lives are inextricably interconnected. The perfectly reasonable material aspirations of China, Brazil or India are consuming limited resources and affecting the prices paid in countries where consumption has been running high for years. The living conditions of people in the mountains of Afghanistan or Pakistan may lead to terrorism in Europe or the USA. The minority in the developed world, or with similar lifestyles elsewhere, consume more resources, take more flights, drive more cars, but everyone feels the impact and effects. Indeed, it is the poorest people of the world—the majority who consume and pollute least—who often feel things most acutely, as with food price rises and, it seems likely, the effects of global climate change. We cannot rest in ignorance. And, to reiterate, with knowledge comes responsibility.

This is the complex global world in which we live, and the world in which our children and students have led most of their lives.

> ► **How does the world now differ from the world in which you were educated?**
> ► **How has education changed?**
> ► **Have the changes in education kept pace with changes in the world?**

Educating for life in a global world

Education has responded to the new global world in a variety of ways. **Multicultural education** is a constellation of responses to the diverse populations of societies and schools associated with globalization. It is concerned with smooth assimilation of ethnic groups to develop a harmonious community and country. Intolerant of racism, it aims to reduce or eliminate stereotyping on ethnic, national or religious grounds, and promotes inclusive pluralism. Non-native speakers are taught the country's lingua franca, while efforts may be made, as in Canada, to maintain students' mother tongues. Cultural and religious diversity is reflected in what all students learn in social and religious studies and the arts, in assemblies, celebrations of different cultural and religious festivals, and in school food. **Intercultural education** is sometimes used to mean the same as multicultural education. However, it can be used more broadly, concerned with any aspect of education for diversity.

> ▶ In what ways does cultural diversity impact on your teaching?
> ▶ What impact does education in culturally mixed groups have on students?
> ▶ Consider your own experience of education in multicultural contexts—in your education and professional experience. What have you learned personally from this?

International education—a term both widely and loosely used (Marshall 2006)—is another response to the global world. In schools, it was originally associated with education for children of globally mobile expatriates in "international schools", and included exported versions of national education. The International Baccalaureate (IB) curriculum, developed in international schools, initially provided education designed for this culturally and linguistically diverse group. Not being rooted in any national educational system, it provides an international perspective.

A debate about whether "international education" and international schools were inextricably linked led to a recognition that international education needed to focus on the curriculum and the process, not the context—particularly when international schools identify themselves as such (see, for example, Hill (2000) and Roberts (2003)). The IB curriculum itself has been widely adopted outside "international schools", and national state schools now form the majority of IB World Schools.

Ian Hill (2007a) describes the concept of international education in the IB Diploma Programme, which embraces:

- educating the whole person with academic breadth and a programme of creativity, action, service (CAS)
- citizenship education via service, preferably in the community external to the school
- critical reflection, dialogue and research skills
- intercultural understanding
- learning more than one language
- lifelong learning: learning how to learn
- values that promote wise choices for the good of humankind.

The IB has formulated a range of devices and initiatives to encourage IB World Schools to develop and exemplify what it calls "international-mindedness", central to which is the IB learner profile (IB 2006a). International education, as seen in the three IB programmes, involves international perspectives and examples because they are seen as intrinsically important and beneficial, whether schools are culturally diverse or not. International education is also pragmatic, equipping students for education and work internationally. It is concerned with values to varying extents, depending on the curriculum body. Other programmes that may be described as international education include the Cambridge International Examinations suite of programmes and the International Primary Curriculum.

Reflection

▶ In what ways does your own teaching incorporate international dimensions?

▶ What impact on students do you aim to have in incorporating international elements?

▶ Reflect on your own experience of multi-/intercultural and/or international education.

▶ Is there a distinct pedagogy or methodology associated with multi-/intercultural and/or international education?

▶ How has your own teaching or administration changed from being involved in multi-/intercultural/international education?

▶ What are the most significant things you have learned from your involvement with international/multicultural classes?

A third educational response to our globalized world is **global education**—concerned with global issues, and with events and perspectives on a global scale. Tye (1999) explored global education, or related fields, in 50 countries. The most common issues studied were ecology/environment, development, intercultural relations, peace, economics, technology and human rights, although he found practice to be very variable. Global education embraces work in the USA and elsewhere under this heading since the 1960s, and parallel work in the United Kingdom (UK) initially described as "world studies" (Hicks 2007a; Burnouf 2004). Earlier work focused on social studies, but the perspective has broadened. Global education also relates to a number of other fields such as peace education, human rights education and the important field of **development education** (see, for example, DEEEP).

The website of the Global Education Centre in New Zealand defines global education as "a process which enables people to understand the links between their own lives and those of people throughout the world. It aims to develop skills, attitudes and values to bring about a more just and sustainable world." The Council of Europe's North-South Centre defines global education as "education that opens people's eyes and minds to the realities of the world, and awakens them to bring about a world of greater justice, equity and human rights for all" (Council of Europe 2002). This is education with an overt ideology.

A number of writers have articulated a theoretical basis for global education, for example, Hanvey (1976) in the USA; Pike and Selby (1988, 1999, 2000) in the UK and Canada; and Hicks (2007a) in the UK. Global education and its related fields are characterized by:

- a focus on those issues that are truly global and run across geographical and political boundaries
- a holistic approach that looks at interdependence and interactions between systems
- recognition that global issues impact on and are affected by all levels, from the local to the global
- recognition that, in global issues, past, present and future are linked; we need to know about the past to understand the present and future; we should have an eye to the future at all times when considering the present
- an openness to other world views and perspectives
- teaching and learning that is participatory, cooperative, exploratory and learner-centred, paying due attention to the rights of the child; embodying an approach that focuses on "exploration of differing value perspectives and which leads to politically aware local and global citizenship" (Hicks 2007b: 25). Although affective elements are important, analysis and critical thinking are also emphasized.

From this brief simplistic consideration of multi-/intercultural, international and global education we can discern three distinct but complementary perspectives—all of which bring something to the table as we consider education for our global world (Table 1.1).

Two other areas of education also relate to education for a global world. **Education for sustainable development**, or, as some prefer, for sustainable living, is a relatively recent response to emerging environmental concerns and economic and social development on a finite planet. **Citizenship education**, educating young people to identify with and play a part in their country and communities, has developed a global dimension, as participation in the "global community" is considered. For international schools with students of diverse national backgrounds mostly living in a foreign "host country", global citizenship is an appropriate vehicle for considering rights and responsibilities in relation to the wider community. (See Urry (1999) for a succinct consideration of the relationship between globalization and citizenship.)

Perspectives in educational programmes		
Intercultural	**International**	**Global**
Concerned with differences and diversity, as well as with underlying common characteristics and features		Concerned with issues that relate to all people, to our common humanity, and with interdependence
Related to characteristics of different cultures (including practices, beliefs and values, languages, religions) Necessarily concerned with human culture	**Related to characteristics of different countries/ nations/states** Concerned with defined parts of the world, and how they differ and interrelate	**Concerned with global issues and systems that relate to all countries and people, across national and regional boundaries: economic, political, environmental, cultural, technological** Concerned with the whole world—all people; the whole planet
Examples of areas of concern and interest		
Different religions, customs and rituals, literature, culture	Political systems of different countries; national economies and their interactions; conflict, trade and relationships between countries	Globalization itself, climate change, finite world resources, global poverty, global infectious diseases

Table 1.1

Key questions

▶ How does your school reflect and respond to cultural diversity?
▶ To what extent, and how, does your school address:
- intercultural/multicultural dimensions?
- international dimensions?
- global dimensions?

▶ How are these dimensions addressed in planning?
▶ Do you have initiatives relating to peace, human rights, sustainable development or other issues-based areas of education?
▶ How does your school address citizenship education?
▶ How do you coordinate between international/intercultural/global dimensions, issues-based education and citizenship education?
▶ How do you assess the effectiveness of your work in these different strands?

Education has certainly been busy responding to the global world with any number of initiatives—often running in parallel (Roberts 2002; Hill 2007b). However, there are some encouraging signs of greater interaction. "International education" in its various manifestations is giving more attention to global issues and dimensions and, in doing the same, some countries are calling on the expertise and experience of those working in global and development education. Can the disparate areas and traditions be brought together in a single and more coherent response? This is the potential of educating for global citizenship.

Schaffer and Thomson's (1992) influential Harvard Business Review paper *Successful change programs begin with results* draws attention to the myriad of change initiatives within business. These can produce a "rain dance"—an "ardent pursuit of activities that sound good, look good, and allow managers to feel good—but in fact contribute little to bottom-line performance".

International, multi-/intercultural, global and development education are examples of "adjectival education". While they may tell us something about what these types of education are *like*, they do not tell us what they are *for*. Educating *for* global citizenship is powerful because it shifts attention away from the activity and process, to the purpose, outcome and result—from the "rain dance" to the "bottom line". We should see global citizens—or better global citizens.

Education for global citizenship synthesizes insights and elements from the various areas of education described. All recognize the importance of empathy, of capacities to see the world through other people's eyes, and, in the words of the IB mission statement, to "understand that other people, with their differences, can also be right". From international and intercultural education come appreciation and understanding of different countries and cultures. Global education provides a focus on issues and concerns that affect people and the planet as a whole, notions of systems and interdependence, and a coherent pedagogy. Global/development education contributes development of ethical and moral responsibility towards our fellow planetary inhabitants, and education for sustainable living provides further emphasis on stewardship of the planet and how human and other species can coexist on it. Citizenship education brings theoretical perspectives and participatory membership of communities—from the local to the global. Drawn together, we have **education for global citizenship**.

This book is about how what we do in schools can be directed towards educating for global citizenship. "What we do in schools" recognizes that there is more to schools, as organizations, than education. But our focus, relentlessly and unremittingly, should be on the young people—the characteristics they show and the changes they undergo. The conferences, the papers, the new initiatives, the school improvement programmes—everything else is a "rain dance" if we do not see impact on the ground, in the young people we work with.

If the global citizen is the "bottom line", then it is important that we know what sort of person he or she is. So, to this we turn.

2 What is a global citizen?

"No local loyalty can ever justify forgetting that each human being has responsibilities to every other."

Kwame Anthony Appiah (2006: xvi)

Activity

▶ What is your *own* personal understanding of the phrase "global citizen" now—at this point?

▶ Write down your own definition or what you understand by the term.

▶ Alternatively, write down words and phrases that come into your mind as you think of the phrase "global citizen".

▶ Don't refer to any materials or look anything up! This exercise is concerned with *your own understanding now.*

▶ Has your understanding of the term changed since you first encountered it?

▶ If so, in what ways, and why?

▶ Do you use the phrase "global citizen" in your vocabulary
  • in normal everyday life?
  • in your professional work?

▶ Do you use another word or phrase in preference, or instead?

Notions of global or world citizenship are not new. Socrates in ancient Greece, Seneca in Rome four centuries later, and Thomas Paine—all have seen themselves as citizens of the world. But such notions engaged the few. Now the "global citizen" is part of popular culture along with globalization and the global village. In part it reflects more fluid relationships between states and their inhabitants. We can live and work for years in countries of which we are not citizens, or become citizens of two or more countries. We may have rights to travel, live and work extending beyond national borders. We are also aware that nation states cannot control everything that affects us. The economy, supplies of resources, even the quality of the air we breathe—all are influenced at a level above the state. We may have loyalties and ties that run beyond countries—to a religion or ethnic group.

We have also developed a sense of the global entity to which we relate. Organizations such as the United Nations (UN) and the International Criminal Court emerged last century with jurisdiction or influence across borders. We have accorded ourselves "human rights" with precedence above national citizenship rights, and we have come to appreciate the whole planet as a "biosphere". China and Russia now play more integrated roles in one highly interconnected world. Various issues, global in scale and requiring global solutions, have emerged and the new millennium was marked by the articulation of the UN Millennium Development Goals representing a global commitment towards all people of the world.

So what could be more obvious than to describe people living in this global world as global citizens? But the term is variably and loosely used. To some it is associated with aspirations for world government and world citizen passports. To some it is a contradiction in terms. To them, as Hannah Arendt argued in the 1960s, "A citizen is by definition a citizen among citizens of a country among countries" (cited in Sweet 2007). Others shun a hackneyed phrase they consider has been casually adopted. Global citizenship has been appropriated by some global companies keen to talk up their ethical and environmental credentials. It is even being used in relation to countries.

Key questions

- ▶ Are the terms "global" or "world citizenship" used in your school? Does the school mission statement, website or brochure refer to "global" or "world citizenship"? Is "global citizenship" used in any curriculum documents that you use?
- ▶ If so, is the term defined in any way? Is its meaning clear from the context?
- ▶ Is there any shared understanding of the term in your school?

If we are educating for global citizenship we need to have a clear understanding of what we mean by "global citizen".

Activity

Consider the way the term "global citizen" is used in the two following contexts.

Huiliang is Chinese, but was born in Malaysia, served in the Red Army, and was a leading scientist in China. After research in the USA and the UK, she settled in the UK permanently. She visits family in the USA, where she also has a home, retains Chinese citizenship, writes academic books in Chinese, and continues to visit China each year on holiday and to lecture. She describes herself as a global citizen.

▶ When used here, what does "global citizen" mean?

Consider now this paragraph from the website of the Victoria International Development Education Association in Australia.

"Citizenship is a term that dates back to the Ancient Greeks. Back then, a citizen was someone who played a role in advancing Greek society. Global citizenship is a new term, but it is based on an ancient concept—a global citizen is anyone who works to make the world a better place."

▶ How global is "global citizenship" in this second piece?
▶ What is the hallmark of a "global citizen" here? How does this differ from the usage in the first context?

Levels of global engagement

Before returning to global citizenship, it is helpful to sidetrack a little here to distinguish between some other "global" terms. These will help clarify our thinking as we move forward. But in this emerging field, be aware that others may use them differently.

Global awareness is concerned with knowledge or everyday experience of the planet and of global issues and concerns. It is to do with *knowing about* things and is a cognitive activity. Global awareness is a necessary base for other types of engagement with the global.

Global understanding implies a higher order appreciation of interconnectedness, systems and processes, but remains cognitive.

Global competence is concerned with knowledge, but more particularly with the skills that enable a person to live and function in different countries and cultures. A person who is globally competent probably speaks several languages, is aware of and can relate to different cultures, and may have qualifications with wide international recognition.

Global competence is a neutral term not associated with any particular attitudes or values. It does not imply ethical behaviour. Indeed, international criminals or mercenaries may show high levels of global competence. Huiliang is globally competent too. She can function well in several quite distinct contexts. In many countries, the need to equip students to earn a living in a globalized world has been receiving increasing attention (for example, from the Council of Chief State School Officers in the USA in 2006). Where this emphasizes the knowledge, understanding and skills needed to operate effectively in a globally competitive world, it overlaps with global competence, as described here.

Global competence may become more important and more common, but it is about functioning in a global world, not about changing it for the better—or even taking responsibility for one's own part in it.

Another approach is to consider how, as individuals, we can engage with the global at various levels. Rogers (1998) researched the changes in adult students during a course on global futures in Canada. She recognized five broad and overlapping dimensions to the changes taking place— effectively a sequence through which students may pass, although not all would move beyond the initial levels (Table 2.1).

Dimensions of learning observed in global issues teaching	
Cognitive	Learning new facts and concepts
Affective	Feelings associated with the new facts and concepts
Existential	Feelings may prompt consideration of deeper issues such as the meaning of life
Empower-ment	If resolved, existential feelings can lead to a sense of personal responsibility and commitment
Action	Informed personal social and political action

Table 2.1

Figure 2.1 is another way of presenting an essentially similar sequence for students engaging with the global. The first level, global awareness, is cognitive. This may lead directly to "caring about" an issue or concern— to do with attitudes and values. In the response to people, it may lead to empathy ("sharing")—an important attribute, which can be shown towards people or fictional characters (and so can be nurtured by studying literature). You cannot care about a fictional character in any meaningful sense: in fictional situations empathy is as far as it gets. Empathy for real people may or may not lead to caring about them. Sometimes empathy for real people also stops at that stage. "Caring about" shows our concern, which may be expressed by talking about it. But in practical terms, "caring about" only has results if it is expressed through action, such as "caring for" people or making a difference in other ways. To many people, the global citizen is engaged, or is working towards engagement at all these levels. Although shown as a linear sequence, actions do, of course, influence our awareness and caring.

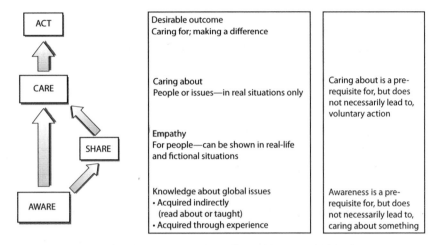

Figure 2.1: Levels of engagement with global issues

Other models express this more simply, as in the following sequences.

- Head, Heart, Hand
- Be aware, Be moved, Be involved (Oxfam UK)
- Knowledge, Compassion, Action (Roots and Shoots youth programme)

To anticipate, educating young people for global knowledge or awareness is quite different from educating for empathy, caring or compassion, or for taking action. The type of global engagement we seek to develop crucially affects the pedagogy and methodology we use.

Global citizenship

Let us return now to global citizenship and look at two more ways of describing a global citizen. The following comes from an article by Belle Wei (2003), a dean at San José State University.

> *"Regardless of whether you realize it, you are a global citizen. The only question is whether you are a successful global citizen. You are a global citizen because you live in a place where what you do and what happens to you is strongly interconnected with what other people are doing elsewhere in the world."*

Compare this with the characteristics of a global citizen, as set out, initially in 1997, by development charity Oxfam GB (2006a).

"Oxfam sees the Global Citizen as someone who:

- *is aware of the wider world and has a sense of their own role as a world citizen*
- *respects and values diversity*
- *has an understanding of how the world works*
- *is outraged by social injustice*
- *participates in the community at a range of levels, from the local to the global*
- *is willing to act to make the world a more equitable and sustainable place*
- *takes responsibility for their actions."*

Reflection

▶ **What are the essential differences between Wei's view and Oxfam's?**
▶ **How do these two understandings relate to ideas of global awareness and global competence?**
▶ **How do these two understandings relate to the levels of engagement in Figure 2.1?**
▶ **Do you consider Figure 2.1 represents your response to global issues?**

Consider each of the elements of Oxfam's global citizen.

▶ **Which do you agree with, and why?**
▶ **If you object to any of these, why is this?**
▶ **If we take Oxfam's definition as the basis for work in school, how would we educate students to promote the development of each of these attributes?**

The statement "is outraged by social injustice" is a particular challenge. (Remember that Oxfam is a non-governmental organization (NGO) working with a particular brief and outlook.)

▶ **Do you consider that this is or should be a characteristic of all global citizens?**

In talking about global citizenship, it is helpful to see the extent to which thinking on citizenship in general is relevant. In political thinking on citizenship, three core components are often recognized:

- rights conferred upon citizens by society
- responsibilities or duties demanded of citizens by society
- membership of a community and an accompanying sense of identity.

For Oxfam's global citizen, rights, responsibilities and identity are also involved. The rights are human rights, asserted for the individual and as an entitlement for all people. Responsibilities and duties are not demanded, but volunteered. Individuals identify themselves as part of the global community—they have "a sense of their own role as a world citizen". Global citizens are also active participants in their communities. Global citizenship is not a neutral status conferred on a passive recipient. Assuming global citizenship on the Oxfam model is active, voluntary and an ethical stand.

This contrasts with the view: "We're all global citizens now, because of the lives we lead, and whether we recognize it or not." There are no right or wrong answers here, but they are very different positions.

The variety of uses of "global citizen" does not end there. The ancient Greeks distinguished between good personal conduct and active participation in civic affairs. To them the latter represented citizenship. Some understandings of the global citizen place emphasis only on ethical personal conduct in a globally interconnected world—on exercising responsible choices as "ethical consumers" or "ethical shoppers", and personal environmental responsibility. To some, active community participation is an optional additional level of engagement. To others it is essential. Others go further, asserting that global citizens must be engaged in trying to change the world by influencing, lobbying or other forms of activism.

Some authors prefer to use other terms, even though their meanings overlap considerably with some understandings of global citizenship. Veronica Boix Mansilla and Howard Gardner (2007) talk of "global consciousness". The important book *Educating citizens for global awareness*, edited by Nel Noddings (2005), talks extensively about global citizenship.

We need to be aware of the fact that people using the same term may mean different things, and those using different terms may mean essentially the same thing.

Conflicts of allegiances and questions of identity

The concept of the global citizen has been criticized for undermining allegiance to the nation state. Rischard (2008) considers: "We must develop new instincts and politics across the planet, whereby each of us is first a global citizen, second a national citizen, and third a local citizen. Right now, we have it the other way around." On such a hierarchical view, there is a potential conflict of allegiances.

This raises the question of our identity. Multiple identities are common. Simultaneously we can be parent, child, teacher, trained biologist and local hockey champion. Some identities we are born with, some we acquire through no effort and others we work hard to acquire. In seeing ourselves as a global citizen we assume another additional identity. Our other identities are not necessarily diminished, but when we see ourselves as a global citizen, we will never see the world in quite the same way again.

> ▶ **What do you consider to be your principal identities?**
> ▶ **How do they affect how you view the world?**
> ▶ **Are there situations where they are in conflict?**
> ▶ **Do you consider your identities to be in any form of hierarchy?**

A note on cosmopolitan citizenship

In the nuanced debate among political theorists on citizenship in a global world, some talk about "cosmopolitan citizenship". This recognizes our relationship as "citizen" to different communities, and avoids attaching a "local", "national" or "global" label. Gunesch (2007) and Osler and Starkey have developed the concept in relation to education. To Osler and Starkey (2005: 78) "cosmopolitan citizenship is a status deriving from equal entitlement to human rights. Importantly, it is based on a feeling of belonging and recognition of diversity across a range of communities from the local to the global."

The term "global citizen" combines two potentially contestable terms and, meaning so many things to different people, it certainly has its drawbacks. The search is on for a better term. Until that time, and for our purposes here, we stay with the term "global citizen", although we need to know what we mean by it.

So what is a "global citizen"?

We need a clear understanding of "global citizen" to direct our activities. What we teach, how we teach and where we teach are very different according to the understanding of global citizen we embrace.

We can take a definition off the shelf, and Oxfam's, as outlined earlier in this section, has been widely adopted or adapted in education circles. But going through the processes of developing our own definition is potentially very productive—as long as we do come out with something clear at the end.

A definition of a global citizen is an important starting point, but it needs elaboration to put flesh on the bones. Here are two examples.

A research team drawn from nine countries (Parker, Ninomiya and Cogan 1999) identified characteristics of citizens they considered equipped for our global world. These included:

- the ability to conceive of problems in global as well as local terms
- the ability to work with others in a cooperative way and take responsibility
- the ability to understand, accept, appreciate and tolerate cultural differences
- the capacity to think in a critical and systematic way
- a willingness to resolve conflict in a non-violent manner
- a willingness to participate in politics at local, national and international levels
- a willingness to change one's lifestyle and consumption habits to protect the environment
- the ability to be sensitive towards and to defend human rights.

This set of attributes would make an excellent elaboration of a basic definition.

Oxfam (2006a) expands on its own definition of a global citizen by proposing key elements of global citizenship, set out under familiar headings.

Knowledge and understanding
- Social justice and equity
- Diversity
- Globalization and interdependence
- Sustainable development
- Peace and conflict

Skills
- Critical thinking
- Ability to argue effectively

- Ability to challenge injustice and inequalities
- Respect for people and things
- Cooperation and conflict resolution

Values and attitudes

- Sense of identity and self-esteem
- Empathy
- Commitment to social justice and equity
- Value and respect for diversity
- Concern for the environment and commitment to sustainable development
- Belief that people can make a difference

Activity

It is now over to you to develop or identify your own understanding of a global citizen—whatever you find helpful at this point in your own situation. You may wish to use Oxfam's definition, or develop your own. It will be helpful to have a written statement to which you can return at various points in the book, and which you may amend as your thinking and understanding develop. This can be done individually, or as a whole school or section. When it comes to global citizenship, all members of the school community have equal status, and it is good to recognize this by ensuring wide participation.

There is plenty of general material available to help thinking. Nigel Dower (2003) gives a philosophical and political introduction and Dower and Williams (eds 2002) compile readings in the field. Hans Schattle (2008) looks at origins and current usage of global citizenship. George Walker's (2006) reflective book *Educating the Global Citizen* includes an elaboration of Martha Nussbaum's ideas in a school context. Its approach is refreshingly different from, and complementary to, Oxfam's bullet points.

A case study of the processes used in one school to embed global citizenship in its core follows.

CASE STUDY

WILLIAM JOHNSTON/ACADEMIA COTOPAXI/QUITO, ECUADOR

Putting global citizenship at the core of a school

Global citizenship is a major part of the mission and vision of the school, which operates on a results-based model. On determining that global citizenship would be a part of the school's core, the board charged the administration with developing a structure for the measurement of the concept.

A task force of staff and students was formed to address the task. Given that the board would have comment and final approval rights and is made up of parents, that stakeholder group was deemed to be represented in the process. The brief was to develop an operational definition of global citizenship, using the school mission, vision and core values as foundation documents, and to include functional rubrics and an evaluation procedure to determine the degree to which the school was meeting its strategic goal of developing global citizens. The work would be periodically reviewed by the administrative team and approved at that level before going to the board for their review, comment and final adoption. With the complexity of the task and the broad range of opinion, it is not surprising that it took a year and a half to arrive at a final document.

The task force decided that the Academia Cotopaxi definition of global citizen would be intimately tied to the degree to which student behaviours demonstrated and reflected the school's core values. As there were no specific, written operational definitions for those values, they began with that task. Each of the values was defined and, as a group, were submitted to the administrative team for review. After substantial discussion and review, the two groups arrived at a set of definitions, which were then submitted to the board.

The task force next moved to defining a global citizen. Following the same process, the group finalized a functional definition and rubrics to guide staff in recognizing and evaluating the desired behaviours.

Assessment activities for the high school were consolidated into a required portfolio, the structure for which was developed by students in conjunction with the technology department. School planned activities range from internal, day-to-day experiences to comprehensive community service. Experiences are not limited to those that the school plans as part of the curriculum, but may involve anything that the student does that can be verified.

Educating for global citizenship

Although the term global citizenship is often used in relation to companies and countries, here we are focused on individuals. The definition of global citizen we shall be using is essentially Oxfam's, with four additional points. A global citizen:

- has a sense of connectedness with and responsibility towards others, other species and the environment
- understands interconnectedness and complexity
- can see the world through the eyes of others
- views the future with hope.

Educating for global citizenship calls for a pedagogy emphasizing active learning, cooperation, critical understanding of global issues, community participation and development of a sense of justice and equity. This emphasis on attitudes, values and participation contrasts with a focus on knowledge and skills. The pedagogy draws on the strong tradition of development education and the approach of the Brazilian educator Paulo Freire (1921–1997). This may require some rethinking and readjustment professionally.

In our work, we need openness and humility. We need to be open to students' perspectives, and to those emerging from other countries and traditions. It would indeed be unfortunate if educating for global citizenship (perhaps particularly in service learning) became an unwitting and actively pursued imposition of post-colonial Western views. So we need to be educating ourselves as global citizens too. (The international professional development project "Through Other Eyes" provides excellent online materials encouraging us to see the world differently.)

We shall be emphasizing action, on the basis that there is little point in studying and knowing about global issues as an end in itself. Throughout the book, when there is talk of "addressing global issues" or similar phrases, it is assumed that the approach is one of global citizenship, moving from awareness to promote caring about the issues, and encouragement to take action.

The rest of the book is concerned with two questions. How can all aspects of school life be directed towards the development of individuals as better global citizens? And, amid our flurry of activity, how do we know individuals are changing, and for the better?

3 The role of schools

Schools have an important and relatively uncontroversial role as society's means of transmitting knowledge and skills to the young. Educating for global citizenship propels schools into a potentially different arena and it is appropriate to raise a few issues and set the scene for subsequent chapters.

Schools as communities

Schools are communities in which teachers and students spend large proportions of their daily lives. If citizenship is about active participation in a community, it needs to start in school. Membership of the global community is a rather diffuse notion, and needs to be grounded in and develop from nurtured participation in the very real school community. Chapter 6 develops this and looks at how students can contribute to decisions and operations in schools.

However, as communities go, schools are somewhat unusual. First, they are disproportionately young. Second, at least some students are there because they must be. Third, relationships between members of the community are uneven. Students and adults have different roles, with the adults usually having more of a say in what happens.

Global co-citizens

"We worry about what a child will become tomorrow, yet forget that he is someone today."

Stacia Tauscher

The uneven relationship between students and teachers in schools is entirely appropriate for transmission of knowledge and skills, and for care and welfare. But global citizenship calls for a reappraisal of roles and pedagogy. Unlike national citizenship, global citizenship involves no acquisition of status on passing a certain birthday and everyone in and associated with schools is in the same position.

Global citizenship is about grappling with the global in our everyday lives, keeping ourselves informed, thinking about the right or just thing to do, and taking action. As teachers, we bring different and better developed intellectual tools and skills, and we have more experience of life. But young people are arguably more immersed in the global world—they have lived their entire lives in it—and some will undoubtedly be better global citizens than some adults. There is another consideration too. Most global concerns have been produced or exacerbated by older people, the people with knowledge and power. The young may be living with these concerns in the world, but their part in causing them is smaller, simply because they have been around for less time.

Besides this, working with and alongside students as equals can be very beneficial educationally—and fun! For all of these reasons, when it comes to working with students in global citizenship, it seems appropriate to do so as equals.

What should schools do—or not do?

Before we become immersed in how we can address global citizenship in schools, this short section raises two basic and potentially controversial issues.

Activity

Read the following passages. The first is by Clayton Lewis, head of Washington International School, and following it is a response from Robert Pierce of Grafton High School, Yorktown, VA, USA.

"An overwhelming body of evidence suggests that our global family finds itself at grave risk, with the increasingly pragmatic realization that our fate is inextricably bound together. Five years into a new century, we face issues that are profoundly different from those of the post Second World War era, particularly in the sense that they cannot be solved by unilateral or even multilateral action, but only through extraordinary cooperation of people worldwide. We have little time to make collective decisions about our current predicament. We as educators have an urgent responsibility to alert young people to new realities that result from globalization and to encourage their wholehearted search for solutions. Remarkably, perhaps tragically, this is not a predominant focus in ... schools."

Clayton Lewis (2006: 51)

The error of reconstructionism

Every generation has doomsday predictions that some educators use to promote particular ideas. When educators rely on fear or extreme cognitive dissonance (psychological conflict or anxiety because of con-tradictions between a person's simultaneously held beliefs or attitudes) to convert students to their (political) agenda, they adopt a philosophy of education known as Reconstructionism. While the label has histori-cally specific origins in the Great Depression, when certain left-wing progressive educators called for radical reconstruction of the social and economic order, the Reconstructionist approach is timeless.

Reconstructionism is morally problematical. At a human level, fright-ening people—unless the threat is unquestionably real and the danger immediate—is a form of psychological abuse. At a professional level, teachers have an obligation to aim at political neutrality. Thus, Recon-structionism is objectionable on two counts: (1) mistreating students (2) for a political end.

Lewis unquestionably has good intentions. What if the threats he is thinking of are real? If so, changing our curriculum should probably not be our highest priority. If, however, the world is not coming to an end, we should not use doomsday predictions as the foundation for our schools nor as the basis for global citizenship (a political position). Today, fostering global awareness is a laudable, arguably necessary, goal, but let us not compromise higher ideals of appropriate treatment of stu-dents and professional integrity in achieving it.

▶   Question: Where do you stand with regard to these two positions?

Key questions

▶ Can addressing global issues in school be entirely neutral politically? Are schools politically neutral by not addressing global issues?
▶ Is global citizenship a political position?
▶ Is global citizenship based on "doomsday predictions"?
▶ Does educating for global citizenship represent education for a political end?
▶ Is the professionalism of teachers undermined by indicating that certain issues, such as climate change, are important and urgent?
▶ How can we address with students issues that appear important and urgent, without causing them anxiety?

Educating for activism?

Michael Byers (2005), a law professor in the University of British Columbia, takes a robust view of global citizenship.

> *"If we're going to talk about global citizenship, let's talk frankly about how and where power vests and is wielded in today's world ... and about the hypocrisies and hollowness of less rigorous or more benevolent conceptions of global citizenship ... Global citizens, whatever they are, can't be content to remain within the narrow, formal constraints of a voting democracy, since democracy of this kind simply doesn't exist on a global level. Whatever global citizens are, they must engage in other manners and forms of democracy, to be activists of some kind."*

Key questions

▶ **Are global citizenship and activism inseparable?**
▶ **Should schools be educating for activism?**

School-wide audits and benchmarks for global citizenship

It helps to have a realistic assessment of the current position before planning future directions and actions. The rest of the book incorporates questions and activities, some of which constitute elements of an audit. However, there are several tools available for schools to assess the extent to which they are addressing international and global dimensions, and one (Oxfam's) specifically for global citizenship. Although developed for specific contexts, all instruments are of relevance, although schools may prefer to devise their own.

In the UK, the Developing Citizenship project *Benchmarks for secondary schools in a global context* addresses three areas: curriculum planning and delivery; creating opportunities for partnerships; and school ethos and policy development. Visit http://www.teachingexpertise.com/files/Secondarybenchmarks.pdf archived at http://www.webcitation.org/5ZqefK2CK.

The International School Award is available to schools in the UK, Sri Lanka and India. Its documentation includes a simple self-audit form to be completed with examples of relevant work within schools. Visit http://www.globalgateway.org.uk/default.aspx?page = 1843.

Global Education Checklist, devised by Fred Czarra in 2002 for the American Forum for Global Education, covers student knowledge, the school, the local school system and state education agencies in the US context. Visit http://www.globaled.org/fianlcopy.pdf archived at http://www.webcitation.org/5ZqeD84kR.

Oxfam Education has a simple audit tool specifically for global citizenship, in which schools assign the extent (Excellent, OK, or Working towards) to which they address 14 key indicators. The format encourages schools to include evidence and action points. Visit http://www.oxfam.org.uk/education/resources/global_citizenship/overall_files/ideas_for_getting_started_and_inspired.pdf archived at http://www.webcitation.org/5ZpDZsseG.

The International Schools Association's comprehensive *Internationalism in Schools: A self-study guide* focuses on internationalism in the international school context. Available for purchase at http://www.isaschools.org. (For a research-based evaluation, see Cambridge and Carthew (2007).)

Yorkshire and Humberside Global Schools Association (YHSA) *Benchmarks of the Global Dimension* is a short document giving indicators under six areas: leadership and ethos; teaching and learning; monitoring and evaluation; resources; staff development; and parental/community involvement. Visit http://www.yhgsa.org.uk/benchmarks.htm.

Research evidence on schools and global (citizenship) education

Research on global education in schools is limited, and on global citizenship education even more so—it is a new field and the research is intrinsically difficult. Cathie Holden (2007a) reports on research in the UK and elsewhere on students' views on social and global issues. Little research has been undertaken on primary school children, although she describes studies she undertook in UK schools in 1994 and 2004. Students in 2004 seemed to be more engaged as active citizens (for example, in campaigns and fund-raising) than students in 1994. This may reflect the impact of the new citizenship curriculum—an encouraging indirect indication that schools may be able to make a difference in this area.

More research has been carried out at secondary level, although still rather limited and principally in developed countries. There is some evidence of students feeling disempowerment, pessimism and disengagement in relation to global issues. However, feelings of despondency about large-scale issues are not necessarily reflected in anxiety and pessimism in students' personal lives.

Holden concludes that work to engage students as global citizens should begin young, while they are enthusiastic and energetic. In the secondary school, time needs to be provided for students to talk about their concerns and to take appropriate action. "Involvement in community action and interest in political and global issues needs to increase, not decrease, as pupils grow older so that as young adults they feel motivated to make a difference" (Holden 2007: 43). How does this relate to actual practice in our schools?

More recently, Ipsos MORI undertook a major study to ascertain the impact of "global learning" on students aged 11 to 16 in England (DEA 2008). Global learning covers all learning involving international or global aspects. Those who had experienced global learning, compared with those who had not, were keener to learn more about global issues, more open to the views of people from different backgrounds and more likely to believe they could do things to make the world a better place.

These research findings are important as they give clear evidence that addressing global and international issues in schools does make a difference to student attitudes and action. It is reassuring to find that what we would hope for and expect is supported by research.

In considering the development of young people as global citizens, the home and life outside school are obviously important. Students come under the influence of others, particularly their parents, and many lifestyle choices are made outside school. Our efforts to educate for global citizenship will be enhanced or diminished by some of these external influences. But we should be motivated and supported in our work to educate young people for global citizenship by knowing that research indicates that what we do is important, and works. With this encouraging background, let us look now in more detail at what we can do.

4 Getting the conditions right

"Don't worry that children never listen to you. Worry that they are always watching you."

Robert Fulghum

Global citizenship education, learning from citizenship education more generally, needs to focus on the "three Cs".

- Taught **C**urriculum
- **C**ulture and ethos
- The wider **C**ommunity—at all levels from the local to the global.

We shall look at the taught curriculum and community involvement in later chapters. This chapter looks at culture and ethos, and how the stage can be set in school for the development of global citizenship. It ranges quite widely, and into byways and backwaters that may not seem immediately relevant to work with students. But young people sometimes see connections that are less obvious to us, and quickly detect if we say one thing and do another.

Let us start with some research findings. Global citizenship education is a new field, so we have to look to other related areas to provide relevant pointers from research. Mary Hayden and Jeff Thompson of the University of Bath (1996, 1997) investigated what those in international schools thought were important features of international education. Questionnaires were issued to students, aged 16–18, to secondary level teachers and to undergraduates who considered they had recently experienced an international education.

Thompson (1998) concluded that in all three survey groups, exposure to students of different cultures within the school was perceived to be the most important factor. We shall consider this conclusion and its implications in greater detail below. Stemming from their research and that of others, Hayden and Thompson (1996) identify five "universals of international education":

- exposure to others of different cultures within the schools
- teachers as exemplars of international-mindedness
- exposure to others of different cultures outside the schools
- a balanced formal curriculum

- a management regime with values consistent with an institutional international philosophy.

In this chapter we shall be considering the importance of diversity within the student body, and the management regime. Consideration of the other "universals" will emerge in subsequent chapters.

The mix of nationalities and cultures within the school

One might expect that a diversity of cultures within a school would be beneficial to the development of global citizenship and some schools, notably the United World Colleges, make efforts to ensure diversity within the student body. But many schools, of course, simply reflect the composition of the local community.

There is some research evidence that a mix of different backgrounds can help to develop more positive attitudes and behaviour towards others. The "contact hypothesis" put forward by Allport (1954) suggests that association between people from culturally different groups may reduce prejudice and conflict and lead to greater liking and respect. There have been hundreds of studies to investigate this over the years, in many contexts. In 2000, Pettigrew and Tropp analysed the research. They concluded that simply having contact between groups reduced prejudice, whether contact was voluntary or not. They suggested that the beneficial effects of contact would be greatest when all aspects of prejudice and stereotyping are addressed, and in longer-term contact situations—such as schools and work—rather than in short encounters. Policies to promote interaction, and situations concerned with change and development, are also helpful.

Schools with a diverse student body are well placed to fulfill all these conditions. They are among the best situations in which prejudice can be reduced. But there is encouraging news for schools with less diverse populations. It has also been found that having a close friend who knows people of a different group can also reduce prejudice and suspicion of that group (reported in Best 2004).

Let us now return to look more closely at Hayden and Thompson's research with students. Their 1997 study identified a cluster of features, which students in "international" schools of different types ranked as particularly important in international education:

- learning in class about other countries (their history, geography, politics)

- learning in class how to consider issues from more than one perspective
- being taught to be tolerant of cultures whose practices are different from one's own
- being taught that all cultures are equally valid
- mixing with students from a number of cultures within classes at school.

Note that it is only the fifth of these features that is undeniably and inextricably linked with cultural diversity in the classroom. A culturally diverse student body may certainly provide favourable conditions for the first four features, but they do not necessarily require this. We can tentatively conclude that while a mix of nationalities and cultures (the context) can be beneficial for developing global citizenship, other features concerned with how we teach and the values we exhibit and promote (the process) are also perceived as important.

This raises the issue of what we mean by diversity in a school. An international school may have an impressive nationality tally, but the student body may be relatively homogeneous in other respects.

Key questions

▶ **How diverse is your school?**
▶ **In what ways does it show diversity?**
▶ **How do you reflect and respond to diversity in your educational provision?**
▶ **What are the implications of the diversity in your school for educating for global citizenship?**

We have seen that superficial contact can reduce prejudice, but in developing global citizens it is reasonable to look for greater cultural engagement. The quality and depth of encounters with different cultures, backgrounds and perspectives—what is sometimes called "the other"—seem likely to be more important than the number of superficial encounters. While a very diverse student or staff body can provide opportunities for such depth of experience, it does not ensure that it will happen. Encounters of equal or greater depth and impact can take place in purposeful and quiet conversations and encounters, and reflections on these, with just one other person who sees things differently—in or out of school.

Governance of the school

By being informed, open, caring, participatory and ethical, boards establish enabling conditions in which global citizens can flourish. They can also play a more direct and active role, initiating or offering overt support to relevant action and activities. Of course the converse also applies. In a school for global citizens the board must be leading or on side.

Key questions

▶ **How would you describe the role and position of the board in relation to the development of global citizenship in your school?**
▶ **Is it neutral, disabling, enabling, discouraging, encouraging?**
▶ **What are the implications of this?**

School mission statement

"When members of a school community, acting as a family, create a mission statement whose purpose is to truly guide their thinking and subsequent behaviours, the lasting effects of these efforts can be monumental", says Douglas Fiore (2001: 35). This suggests that the value of a mission statement is in the process of formulating it. But school communities change and we cannot produce mission statements every year. What of those who play no part in its formulation? Davis et al (2007) investigated whether mission statements had any influence on university students who had played no part in their creation. The researchers suggested that inclusion of ethical content in the mission statement did influence the ethical orientation of students.

Experience in the IB supports this. The IB learner profile appears to have had considerable impact on thinking and practice in IB World Schools. Yet its origins lie outside the IB, devised by a group of innovative primary school teachers. Forming part of what later became the IB Primary Years Programme, the learner profile was adapted and adopted for all IB programmes. This suggests the possibility of a well-drafted and challenging mission statement having similar impact in schools, on those who played no part in its development.

Cambridge (2003) distinguishes between "internationalist" and "globalist" aspects in international school mission statements. Internationalist elements are concerned with *idealism and ideology* in relation to international and global dimensions, while globalist elements relate to *instrumental* considerations.

"Internationalist" elements are associated with:

- education as a process not a product (such as a qualification)
- the development of personal character and values
- expression and development of values including a commitment to world peace, understanding between nations and responsible world citizenship.

"Globalist" elements are associated with:

- viewing education as a product, not a process
- education that facilitates global movement of young people between schools by transferable certification
- globally recognized quality assurance of schools, curriculums and assessments.

Activity

Look again at your school mission statement—or equivalent for your school.

▶ Can you recognize "internationalist" and/or "globalist" elements in any parts that are concerned with living in a global world?

We might expect a school committed to developing global citizens to say this in its mission statement.

An increasing number of schools get this far. Fewer get further. Given that global citizenship means different things to different people, a written elaboration of the school's own understanding of a global citizen is helpful. It then needs to permeate all our activities in all areas.

School ethos or climate

School ethos is an important but rather nebulous concept. *Citizenship education at school in Europe* (Eurydice 2005) describes it in the following terms: "School culture—also known as the 'ethos' or 'general atmosphere' or 'climate' of a school—may be defined as its system of attitudes, values, norms, beliefs, daily practices, principles, rules, teaching methods and organizational arrangements." Ethos impacts on the behaviour of the whole school community, affects its interactions with the wider community and how it faces challenges. The ethos of a school can be positive and life-affirming—or not. Although difficult to pin down, we can certainly sense the ethos when we spend time in a school.

A positive ethos is characterized by:

- a strong sense of community
- good caring relationships between all members of the community
- a safe nurturing environment
- a welcoming, inclusive atmosphere
- positive links with the wider community.

Carlsson-Paige and Lantieri (2005) identify some additional conditions for environments in which social responsibility in young people is nurtured, and which would certainly apply to our schools for global citizens:

- participation in decision-making and pro-social behavior
- modelling of pro-social and ethical behaviour by adults
- development of skills such as perspective-taking and conflict resolution
- opportunities to confront injustice.

Ensuring a peaceful and peaceable school environment is essential for global citizenship education, as for much else. Conflict resolution skills are learned, and research indicates that without training many students never learn such skills (Johnson and Johnson 1996). Some schools find benefit in using an established conflict resolution programme. Those that have been researched and found to be effective include the Resolving Conflict Creatively Program (RCCP), studied by Selfridge (2004), or Teaching Students to be Peacemakers (TSP) (Stevahn 2004). The TSP programme can be incorporated into curriculum work, and involves a number of elements including:

- developing cooperative conditions
- defining and identifying conflict
- teaching negotiation and mediation procedures
- resolving real conflicts.

CASE STUDY

Reed Rhodes/Beijing City International School/China

Hats on for peace

Edward de Bono's thinking tool "Six Thinking Hats" distinguishes hats of six colours, each associated with a particular thinking approach, "worn" as appropriate.

The kindergarten students in Ms Vimla's class were ready for recess and dutifully queued up by the door. As Rocky stood in the doorway waiting his turn to go out, Matheus pushed him from behind causing him to fall forward and rip his jeans and bruise his knee. At home his parents asked him what had happened. Reluctantly, he related the events. When asked, "What did you do to fix the problem?" he hung his head. It was clear that he did not have the tools to deal with the student who had pushed him.

The next day Rocky's mother talked to his teacher, who consulted the learning support (LS) teacher to find a way to empower her students to resolve conflicts. The LS teacher joined the morning circle in Ms Vimla's classroom and introduced the Six Thinking Hats to the class. Students learned about the type of thinking associated with each hat through a picture, a gesture and a cheer. The students sang a song that incorporated the gestures and cheers. Once the students had learned the type of thinking associated with each hat, the LS teacher focused on the white-red-green-blue sequence of hats to resolve conflicts. The white hat along with its gesture (opening a book) is used to state the facts— "You pushed me through the doorway." The red hat along with its gesture (pointing to your heart) is used to state feelings—"I feel angry and sad when you do that." The green hat along with its gesture (arms outstretched like tree branches) is used to generate new ideas to fix the problem—"Next time instead of pushing me, wait your turn to go out so no one gets hurt." The blue hat along with its gesture (waving a conductor's baton) is used to gain consensus about a plan—"Is that OK with you?" After that intervention, whenever her students approach her to solve a conflict, Ms Vimla tells them, "Use your Thinking Hats!"

CASE STUDY

NAJELAA SHIHAB/SEKOLAH CIKAL/JAKARTA, INDONESIA

Conflict resolution in the classroom and beyond

Teachers in Cikal have conflict resolution training at the beginning of each academic year. We plan at least one IB Primary Years Programme unit of inquiry in alternate years that focuses on this issue, and we develop peer mediators. Training for teachers and staff revealed that a lot of teachers in the school do not realize that they have a natural inclination *not* to solve conflict. One teacher said, "I realize that being submissive does not really solve my family problem. Instead it hides a time bomb that could lead me to aggression."

During a unit of inquiry, "Two sides of a story", students examined the nature of conflict. Discussion of "approach-approach conflict", where they chose between two likable things, made students realize that conflict does not necessarily mean negative experiences and is actually a very big part of their daily activities. A year 4 student was motivated to exclaim, "I know now that conflict is not something bad that we should avoid, but something good, because we can learn from it."

At the beginning, teachers had some doubt about implementing the peer mediator programme for a very young age group (ages 7–10) since understanding different perspectives and reflecting on one's own feelings can be very challenging, even for adults. It turned out to be a very rewarding experience, for all parts of the community. A mother told the school proudly that she had been learning the power of using an "I message" with her husband, after observing her child using it with a younger sibling.

Ethos is too complex and all-pervading to be easily summed up. But identifying what the school considers important in easily memorized form can articulate and promote the ethos. Schools belonging to the Round Square organization, based on the influential work of Kurt Hahn, embrace six pillars or precepts encapsulated in the word IDEALS: Internationalism, Democracy, Environment, Adventure, Leadership and Service, which students make a commitment to address. For more information visit the Round Square website at http://www.roundsquare.org.

Management

The importance of the values of the management regime is recognized in its appearance as one of Hayden and Thompson's "universals" of international education. In our school for global citizens, we would expect management, like governance, to be informed, open, consultative and participatory. We would also expect a clear commitment to the concept of global citizenship, expressed not only in words, but in how people spend time and money and establish priorities. Management needs to make sure that the right things happen.

Key questions

Consider the ethos of your school.

▶ **Can you identify what features are more positive, and which less positive?**

▶ **Can you think of any specific practical suggestions for ways in which ethos could be enhanced to better enable educating for global citizenship?**

▶ **Does management show clear support for global citizenship, or for the conditions that promote it?**

▶ **Is there a responsibility post for global citizenship/global issues within your school?**

▶ **Is there a budget for resources relating to global citizenship?**

Policies, procedures and operations

The mission statement needs to be carried through the school in its policies, procedures and operations. First and foremost is a commitment to global citizenship education in the curriculum policy. Oxfam's audit (as discussed in chapter 3) considers that equal opportunities and behaviour management policies are also necessary. An equal opportunities policy sets out the school's commitment to treat all people equally, irrespective of differences relating to specified characteristics. A behaviour management policy sets out comprehensively the methods used in shaping and developing student behaviour, as well as the underlying thinking.

Schools committed to educating for global citizenship should also reflect this in their general operations and activities. So, depending on the context, we might expect to see:

- an environmental policy affecting all the school's activities (for example, a commitment to reduce use of resources, to reuse or to recycle)
- an ethical sourcing policy, relating to the ethical and environmental operations of suppliers of goods and services

(implemented, for example, by selecting a school bank with an ethical investment policy; using fair trade goods; using meat, fish and timber that are sustainably produced or sourced)

- an energy policy (for example, using "green" sources of renewable energy; setting out conditions under which heating and air conditioning are used and the temperature at which the school is maintained).

It is important not to turn a blind eye to what is happening in our schools, even in areas not directly under our control. For example, we may use external contractors for some of our services. What are the conditions of the people who clean our schools, or prepare our food, under a contract? Do they receive a reasonable wage? What materials are they using in cleaning? What are their effects?

Having policies and procedures in place does not mean they are implemented. But these are the nuts and bolts of the school's ethos, and they require the commitment of the school board and management. Of course, implementing all these will not ensure development of global citizens. But failure to adopt or implement can raise issues of credibility, and help to disable their development.

School building and grounds

The building itself

Ideally, schools would be built according to the best sustainable development practice. The new Green School in Bali, for example, is constructed of bamboo, mud and the local alang-alang grass. For most schools the building is a given. However, all schools can undertake audits to see how buildings can be improved to reduce energy use, to conserve heat, or to incorporate green (living) roofs.

Building operations (heating, lighting, waste)

It is often people who have not been involved in formulating policies or procedures who actually perform key operations within a school. Implementation will work best if they are involved in discussions or, at least, if the reasons for the policies and procedures are explained. Resources may also be needed to ensure compliance.

If the school has an **energy policy**:

- can teachers actually control the temperature of their classrooms, and avoid opening windows simply to lose heat?

- who orders things such as batteries? Are rechargeable batteries used rather than disposable ones?

If there is a **transport policy**:

- are students encouraged to walk to school?
- are cycle racks provided?
- are there showers for staff who cycle long distances to school?
- is car use by staff, parents and students encouraged/enabled or discouraged?

If there is an **environmental/recycling policy**:

- is there a way of ensuring that ordering takes account of the policy?
- is there someone whose job it is to check that waste is being sorted for recycling?
- is there effective monitoring of compliance by manual staff?

Are people in charge of purchasing made aware of the background to key policies and procedures? Are manual staff educated about the importance of their activities and the reasons for policies and procedures? (Lifelong learning can apply to the school kitchen or maintenance staff too.)

Gardens and grounds

Gardens and grounds deserve particular attention, whatever their size. Schools are stewards of the land they occupy and we should take that responsibility seriously.

School grounds can be used for overtly educational purposes, and managed to reflect the school's concern for the environment. Grounds can be cared for in ways that encourage and sustain wildlife, with habitats provided for indigenous species. Non-renewable materials can be avoided or used with care, and plants can be sourced from nursery-raised stock not collected in the wild. Giving students experience of producing their own food has many educational benefits, and helps to connect them with the earth and develop a notion of sustainability. This will be a feature of Green School in Bali. The more general benefits of school grounds are the concern of Learning through Landscapes in the UK (http://www.ltl.org.uk) and Learnscapes (http://www.learnscapes.org) in Australia. Bell and Dyment in Canada have considered how they can be used to promote physical activity.

We need to be vigilant about sourcing. Recent press coverage in Europe has highlighted that some paving stone used in gardens is Indian sandstone.

Working conditions in quarries are poor, and up to 25% of workers are believed to be children, some as young as 6 (Ethical Corporation). It would indeed be a sad irony if materials obtained in such a way were used in a school educating other youngsters as global citizens.

Environmental responsibility, eco-schools and sustainable schools

It is very obvious that schools for global citizens must take environmental responsibility seriously. More recently, concerns for sustainability have come to the fore. Sustainability is broader than environmental responsibility. The standard definition of sustainable development remains that of the Brundtland Report: "development that meets the needs of the present without compromising the ability of future generations to meet their own needs" (World Commission on the Environment and Development 1987). Many prefer now to talk of sustainability rather than sustainable development. In addition to environmental protection, sustainability is also concerned with economic conditions and social equity.

Initiatives to promote greater environmental responsibility and sustainability in schools abound. One of the largest programmes is Eco-Schools, involving over 21,000 schools worldwide. The programme includes classroom study and practical action, and sometimes operates under a local name. Students are encouraged to play an active role in taking practical steps to reduce the environmental impact of the school. A "green flag" is awarded to schools with high achievement in their programme (http://www.eco-schools.org).

The Sustainability Hub links to green school initiatives in many countries (http://www.sustainability.ceres.org.au/files/sei_links_intlssi.htm). These include some that are concerned with environmental responsibility, and others that set this in a broader context. Compare the websites for the Australian Sustainable Schools Initiative, the Gobar Times Green Schools Programme in India, the Green School project in China (Centre for Environmental Education and Communications) and Enviroschools in New Zealand to get an idea of the diversity and richness of initiatives.

Several countries have launched significant initiatives on **sustainable development education** embracing all elements of sustainability and related to UNESCO's decade with this focus. The Australian government's *Educating for a Sustainable Future* (Curriculum Corporation 2005) addresses areas intrinsic to global citizenship education, such as diversity and values and lifestyle choices, and is admirably succinct and practical. In England and Wales, a government "Sustainable Schools" initiative takes a very broad view of "sustainable", promoting health, respect for children's rights, and emphasizing high standards of achievement in all areas. The framework draws direct links with global citizenship. WWF UK has developed a practical guide for schools with a series of activities to be undertaken by teachers individually or in groups. Developed in and for the UK context, it could be used much more widely. The US Partnership for Education for Sustainable Development's student learning standards (2008) are also excellent.

Key questions

▶ **Does your school have a commitment to sustainability?**
▶ **If so, how is this expressed and acted upon?**
▶ **If not, why is this?**
▶ **Does your school take part in any established schemes to promote sustainability?**
▶ **How can your school become more sustainable—in the short term? In the longer term?**
▶ **What are our responsibilities for educating students about sustainable lifestyle choices in their lives outside school?**

Schools for global citizens must be interested in initiatives concerned with sustainability in schools and are encouraged to pursue these vigorously.

Reflection

▶ **How important is it for individuals to be committed to sustainable living in their personal lives, if they are working in a school for global citizens?**
▶ **What areas of global citizenship education are not included in education for sustainability?**

CASE STUDY

Matthew Vallis/Gyeongnam International Foreign School/Sacheon, South Korea

The carbon neutral challenge

In a school catering for children in a small nursery unit through to students in year 12, awareness of global issues was high, but little was being done to find solutions. To answer the challenge "How can a school create a meaningful and effective grassroots programme to counter carbon emissions and global warming?", in winter 2006–7, Sue George and Sally Neaves developed the Carbon Neutral Challenge (CNC). The CNC is a collective effort (for groups of students or whole classes) with a competitive element to stimulate enthusiasm. It focuses on local issues and initiatives, is linked to the curriculum and open to all classes.

Launched each year in a whole-school assembly, students are given ideas and suggestions of activities to help reduce emissions, including whole-school campaigns, class projects, postcard series, persuasive essays, T-shirt designs, music videos and art pieces. Students can participate in any way— as long as the emphasis is on local solutions.

Students have thrown themselves wholeheartedly into the event and produced some innovative and effective local solutions. Among these are the humorously named yet effective "Pee-in-the-Dark Campaign"; the school roof-top garden; and the banner bag project using recycled banners. Responding to interest generated, a new integrated subject "Horticulture, environment and sustainability" has been developed, open to years 5–12. This focuses on organic gardening, seasonal cooking, local solutions to problems and general environmental concerns. Wildly popular with the students, it has launched other environmental endeavours around the school and within the community.

An attitudinal shift has occurred in the whole school community, with students actively seeking out ways to reduce their carbon footprints. Lights, heating and air conditioning are used only when deemed absolutely necessary. There has also been a flow-on effect to other areas of environmental concern, and awareness has spread to students' homes, resulting in changes in food consumption, travel patterns and beyond!

CASE STUDY

GLENIS PAUL/SHA TIN COLLEGE/HONG KONG, CHINA

Sha Tin College Environment Action Group

Sha Tin College Environment Action Group (STC EAG) is a new group that has set out to alter the perceptions and behaviours of the STC community towards living sustainably. Task groups of year 12 student leaders and group members from years 7–11 work on different projects. All projects need to be positive environmentally, socially and economically and have the goodwill of board, staff and students. Cultural beliefs should be respected, and the ecological footprint minimized.

"The EAG works hard to motivate and inform the school of our aims," according to leaders Annie and Chrystina. "Recently our cafeteria has moved from reusable plastic plates to metal utensils. We have an action plan to cut the emissions of the school buses and have been promoting fair trade goods to staff and students. Our 10% initiative is going to be a huge task; we are trying to cut electricity usage by 10% within Sha Tin College. Some of the old habits have stuck tight. A few people do not see the change an individual can make or refuse to accept the impact we can have. Our views could not be more different. Each individual can make a difference. It is all about whether you choose to."

The garden group reused bamboo, car tyres and polystyrene in making a roof-top garden. They are looking at how to reduce the ambient temperature of the classrooms below and enjoyed their first crop of vegetables. Another group collects items from the school community to reuse in other countries.

Students have opportunities to put into practice the theoretical skills learned in regular subjects and are gaining first-hand experience of the highs and lows when trying to change conservative attitudes and systems in people and businesses. Perhaps the most important and lasting change has been within the attitudes of the EAG students. They are much more aware of how their choices have far-reaching consequences for other communities—from farmers working in Tai Po, Hong Kong, and the local bus company, to workers in the coffee fields in Africa. If these students can change the awareness of their classmates, teachers and family members while at school they will take with them the ability to effect change in their new communities.

A commitment to global citizenship education should certainly be expressed in a school's mission statement. But what happens in the school should demonstrate that it is not only expressed, but meant and ensured. In that well-worn phrase, as schools we must not only "talk the talk" but also "walk the walk". And remember ... the students—such admirable detectors of cant—are always watching us.

Key questions

▶ In terms of setting the scene for your work with young global citizens, have you got the conditions right?

▶ Are there any aspects of the school that you consider could be particularly beneficial or detrimental to students' development as global citizens?

5 Events and occasions

In educating for global citizenship, arranging special events or occasions or slanting regular events can be a good place to start. Making global issues the subject of regular events is comparatively simple to arrange, and fits within the timetable. Special events can be arranged in place of regular lessons, but can be accommodated without the challenges of permanent timetable changes. When imaginatively and carefully arranged, such events can have considerable impact, although this is clearly enhanced if they form part of a more comprehensive and coherent approach. But care is needed. The Developing Citizenship project in schools in England found that some superficial one-off events entrench rather than challenge existing stereotypes.

Here we are considering events within school. Activities outside school are addressed in chapters 10 and 11.

The UN has a number of designated days that focus on specific issues, around which assemblies and special days can be based. These include:

March 22: World Water Day

April 22: Earth Day

June 20: World Refugee Day

September 21: International Day of Peace

October 17: International Day for the Eradication of Poverty

November 20: Universal Children's Day

December 1: World AIDS Day

December 10: Human Rights Day

A comprehensive list of international days, years and significant anniversaries can be found at: http://www.un.org/events/index.html. (**Background Information > Conferences and observances**).

Assemblies

Assemblies are a very public way of demonstrating the importance of global citizenship to the school. Formats and activities can include games, role plays, drama, music, visiting speakers, videos or films, displaying materials from websites, readings and student presentations. Assemblies provide opportunities to respond to UN days, to news items or to incidents of importance within the school, locally, nationally or internationally, and to anniversaries of significant people and events. They can also be used to recognize important dates for students from different cultures such as national days, or religious festivals.

Assemblies can be an ideal opportunity for quiet reflection, which can be very powerful when undertaken collectively. The impact on students can be enhanced by their involvement in the delivery and, more particularly, in the preparation of assemblies. Best practice also ensures that there are opportunities to follow up matters raised in assemblies in other contexts—in classes, tutor group/home room periods or at registration times. Building in self-assessment can also be valuable (see chapter 12).

Young and Commins (2002) include a number of suggestions for global citizenship assemblies for primary schools. Assemblies are mandatory in the UK, and so UK websites and organizations are a valuable source of materials. For some ideas specifically on global citizenship in assemblies, visit http://www.oxfam.org.uk/education/resources/global_citizenship/assembly_ideas. Other development agencies such as the Red Cross, WWF and UNICEF also publish assembly materials on their website. Oxfam Education (http://www.oxfam.org.uk/education) aims to post assembly materials on large-scale "natural" disasters within a few days.

CASE STUDY

Constance McGuire/Shanghai American School/China

A Chinese New Year assembly

We have bi-monthly assemblies that focus on our expected school-wide learning results. For the global-minded assembly, which fell around Chinese New Year, our Chinese department, under the leadership of teacher Wendy Da, took on responsibility for planning a variety of Chinese-themed activities to present to the student body. Students in the Chinese language classes gave demonstrations of Chinese calligraphy, Chinese folk dances and the ever-popular lion dance, while our student MC introduced and described each activity. And, to finish it off in style, the Chinese teachers greeted each student leaving the auditorium with a hongbao, the traditional red envelope that children receive at this time of the year.

▶ How can assemblies be arranged and designed to have maximum impact on attitudes and values relevant to global citizenship?

▶ How can full use be made of assemblies as collective activities?

▶ How can students be encouraged to reflect on the input provided in assemblies?

▶ What opportunities are there for following up on matters that arise in assembles in other teaching contexts?

▶ If assemblies are used to help in educating for global citizenship, how can their effectiveness be assessed?

International/global days

Replacing regular teaching with a day specifically on international or global issues gives opportunities to address them more fully. Days can focus on a particular country, a religion, aspects of global issues (water, oil, poverty, natural disasters, food, human rights) or a theme (celebrating diversity, interdependence, sustainability). Learning opportunities abound and students enjoy working in a different way. Such special days also provide opportunities to use a pedagogy best suited to global citizenship education (see chapter 7). At their best they can be memorable and transforming experiences.

The challenge in any short or occasional "international" event is to go beyond the "Fs" (food, fashion, famous people, folklore, festivals) and to remember some of the lessons of multicultural education such as avoiding stereotyping and exoticizing. The culture iceberg model (Schein 1992; Weaver 2000), illustrated in Figure 5.1, reminds us that many important aspects of culture are "submerged". "Surface culture"—the visible part of the iceberg—includes artifacts, visible customs and aspects of folklore. Below this is a middle level of what Schein calls "espoused values". These are consciously held values and beliefs. The middle section of the iceberg bobs up and down in the water, and this part may be visible at times, and submerged at others. The lowest and deepest section of the iceberg is always submerged. This is "deep culture"—those basic assumptions and values that are largely unconscious, but nevertheless important in determining many aspects of our behaviour. Surface culture is a small fraction of total culture—much being at the deep level.

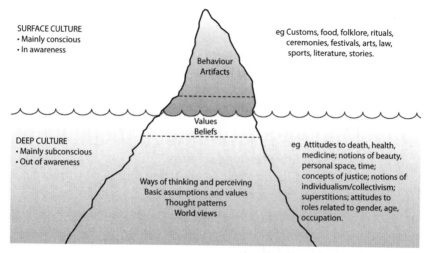

Figure 5.1: What's below the surface? The "iceberg model" of culture (after Schein (1992) and Weaver (2000))

▶ How can we encourage students, and how can we ourselves try to go beyond the observable aspects of culture to the important deeper aspects?

▶ What does the surface culture of your school say about the deeper underlying culture?

Suggestions for global and international days

- Involve parents, NGOs, members of the local community with stories or relevant knowledge/experience (for example, a refugee, someone who has lived in a conflict zone).

- Involve musicians, storytellers, dancers, artists from different cultural traditions—briefed to discuss with students the cultural background and significance of their arts.

- The school community can be a terrific resource for intercultural understanding. Research has shown that prepared, structured one-to-one interviews between students, or by a student of another member of the community (for example, a teacher or other staff member, a parent) can promote cultural awareness and understanding (Pandit and Alderman 2004). Special days may provide opportunities to undertake these, which may not fit into subject classes.

- Encourage reflection. Incorporate a silent period. Encourage students to reflect as they participate in the day, rather than simply providing feedback at the end.

- Consider planning for flexibility, so that the course of the day can take into account students' views collected and expressed during the day. This requires very careful planning.

- Food can be important. Sampling food from different countries and cultures is enjoyable but we can explore deeper culture too: the role of food in the culture and customs of the country and what that says about underlying attitudes towards food and social interaction; food taboos and customs—what different countries eat and do not eat, and the reasons for this; how foods are produced and prepared in the country concerned; food waste and what happens to it in different countries.

- A box of cultural artifacts (or photos) can be provided to a group of students, who then draw what conclusions they can simply from interpretation of these artifacts—a valuable exercise in attempting to understand other cultures, and in the interpretation of evidence. A similar activity can also be done with short videos of examples of behaviour in different cultures. (Visit the website http://www.oxfam.org.uk/education/teachersupport/cpd for advice on using artifacts in teaching for global citizenship.)

- Produce notes or web pages "About our country" to explain aspects of culture to others.

- Investigate and document the country of origin of everything used during the course of a day. Mark countries on a map. Follow up by investigating the origins of some of the items or materials more fully, and the conditions under which they are produced and transported.

- "The World in our Backyard" international day for students aged 7–14 involves researching where everyday items are produced, associated waste production, and devising a game (visit http://www.glade.org).

- Include action—plant a commemorative tree; plant food plants; look at ways of conserving water in school; write letters about an issue of concern to local or national politicians.

- For suggestions on how to observe the UN International Day of Peace in schools visit http://www.internationaldayofpeace.org/.

In-school conferences

For secondary students conferences lasting one day or longer can be of great value. They offer students the opportunity to share or take the lead in organization, in deciding on topics, inviting and introducing speakers and chairing discussions. For students used to working within subjects, they provide opportunities to engage in cross-curricular work. It is again possible to focus on making an impact on students' perspectives, values and attitudes.

George Walker (2007) considers that the most productive conferences/gatherings are when people are engaged in producing something. Student conferences offer the opportunity to break the mould, rather than simply inducting young people in polite audience behaviour.

CASE STUDY

KEITH ALLEN/IBSCA (IB SCHOOLS AND COLLEGES ASSOCIATION, UK AND IRELAND)

Global issues conferences

From 2000, a series of global issues conferences was organized for post-16 students. Each was a kaleidoscope of small-group sessions ("workshops") on a particular issue, mixing students from different schools. Sessions were highly interactive (students feel that they are "told" enough). Each event ended with groups of participants who had attended different workshops. Here, they reported on their learning, discussed their ideas and synthesized common views.

We learned as we went along . A "big name" speaker increased passivity. Resource-led workshops—examining documents, data and presentations—needed a lot of time. Effective sessions often contained a blend of information and discussion. Teachers were good at eliciting discussion, but it was felt that greater "expertise" in the issue would have been beneficial. But "experts" in groups could turn workshops into lectures—and information could easily be pitched at the wrong level. The key seemed to be careful selection and briefing of expert presenters, and allocation of teachers to workshops in which they had some interest, knowledge and understanding of the issue so that they could mediate between students' needs and the presenter's understanding.

Some of the most successful workshops involved presenters with personal stories to tell—a woman rescuing youngsters from child labour, a student activist imprisoned for campaigning against the authoritarian regime in his country, and a 17-year-old with his own business promoting renewable energy systems in the developing—or what is sometimes called the "majority"—world.

Almost invariably, student interaction and engagement had grown during each conference. This reinforced the need for an effective start-up, with ice-breakers to overcome initial reticence. The final session needed careful structuring. Students liked to share their views, but wanted them to be heard. Hence, each final group recorded their thoughts, which were then circulated to participating schools after the conference. Student feedback was also analysed and distributed after the event.

Special events were not going to solve the challenges facing the world, but they could open eyes and ears, minds and hearts.

Theme weeks and months

These may involve replacing the normal timetable with a special programme, perhaps for a week, or giving an emphasis within the regular timetable to particular issues. Impact is strongest when the theme is addressed in all subjects and aspects of school activities. They are therefore easier to implement with primary and lower secondary students than in contexts where syllabus coverage and examinations loom.

I'Anson et al (2005) have compiled good practice and suggestions on "global focus weeks" in primary schools. They recommend having clear concepts to address, and suggest interdependence, sustainability, social justice and diversity. The focus can be on specific countries (one country for the school, or each class focusing on one country and pooling perspectives later), a theme focus (water, food, living together, one world) or a focus on arts or books. Many of the suggestions for special days also apply here, but the more extended period calls for considerable planning (visit http://www.developingcitizenship.org.uk/curr_org_week.htm archived at http://www.webcitation.org/5Yrqmm776 for one school's suggested time plan).

CASE STUDY

Judith Shorrocks/Academia Británica Cuscatleca/El Salvador

Global awareness month

This was a four-week initiative to raise awareness of global issues in middle school students and to provide opportunities for the school's International Global Citizen's Award (IGCA) pilot students to inform their peers and raise funds. (See chapter 13 for more information on the IGCA.)

During the first week, in a 15-minute registration time each morning, tutors showed prepared PowerPoint® presentations explaining what was meant by being more globally aware. Students were asked to pledge to buy an energy-saving light bulb, a reusable shopping bag or a tree to plant. The school had organized someone to make the bags, price up the bulbs, and had found someone to donate the trees.

During the second week, pledge forms were sent home and returned with money. IGCA students promoted the event through posters and in assemblies and went round the tutor rooms each morning explaining, encouraging commitment and collecting pledges from fellow students.

The goods were purchased during the third week, and distributed during the last week.

Earlier, the school had approached the local authority, which designated a local area where IGCA students could plant trees if students did not want to plant them at home.

In retrospect, the whole school should have been involved, not just the younger students. Many families already had energy-saving light bulbs and so that was not a good option. There should also have been cheaper options for some families. Next time, the tutors will expect the IGCA students to be more involved in the initial preparation and promotion of the event rather than just assisting in the running of the event.

Taking part in events and activities organized by others

A number of projects enable students to join global initiatives relating to global awareness or action. Here are a few suggestions of projects that can be undertaken within a school without contact with other schools. Chapters 9 and 10 consider projects that involve working with partner or link schools.

Life Link Friendship Schools

This is a Sweden-based NGO, offering over 50 small-scale projects. Schools can issue certificates to participants, and log participation on the organization's website: visit http://www.life-link.org.

IB global lessons

IB World Schools were invited to teach a lesson on global poverty in October 2008 around World Poverty Day. Outline lesson plans were provided on the IB community theme website (http://communitytheme.ibo.org), but schools could develop and post their own. Students, parents and teachers took part in discussion forums on the IB's community theme website. It is expected that further global lessons will be offered.

Newsday

Students write news articles and post them on the web. They read those of other schools and compile a newspaper of articles from around the world. This is just one of several programmes from GlobalSchoolNet.org: visit http://www.globalschoolnet.org/gsh/project/newsday.

Events and occasions have the potential to make a significant impact on students. (In what ways? How can we know?) But a school committed to education for global citizenship will go much further, as the following chapters elaborate.

6 Student participation

Participating in their communities, at all levels up to the global, is an essential feature of active global citizens. But community participation begins in school, where students can contribute to decisions and operations, and unfolds and extends from there. The case for increasing student participation in schools can be made on three fronts. The first is from research, which leads to some clear conclusions. The International Association for the Evaluation of Educational Achievements (IEA) investigated how young people in 28 countries are prepared for citizenship in democracies. A principal finding was that schools that practise democracy by encouraging students to participate actively in the life of the school are most effective in promoting civic knowledge and engagement. Davies (2006: 14) concluded in another research review that: "the two best school-based predictors of whether people become active citizens (engaged in voluntary work or activism) are: (a) involvement in school democracy and (b) experience of doing some form of community service."

With very little research on global citizenship education specifically, we have to extrapolate from research on citizenship more generally and assume that active participation in the global community will arise because the practice, habit and experience of participation begins young, begins local, begins small, and extends from there. In addition to the effects of student participation on wider community engagement later, there is considerable evidence (see later in this chapter) that student participation brings immediate benefits to the student and the school.

The second argument is that participation is a legal right of young people, as set out in Article 12 of the United Nations Convention on the Rights of the Child (1989). But nuanced interpretations mean this is not clear-cut (Ackerman et al 2003).

The third is a moral issue. Johnson (2004a: 2), speaking from a primary perspective, comments: "There is an emerging body of literature that repositions even young children as competent, active agents who demonstrate considerable insight into, and control over, their daily lives. In re-conceptualizing children in these terms, a strong moral argument emerges for recognizing children's entitlement to a fair say in their own affairs."

Participation of students in their schools seems an essential element of educating for citizenship, global or otherwise. The question is not whether, but how this participation should take place. But first, let us sharpen up our understanding of "participation".

What is student participation?

"Student participation" is used in different ways. In the classroom context it indicates active learning. Here we are focusing on a rather more circumscribed notion of participation—ways in which students contribute to the operations and running of schools. Roger Hart (1992) devised a "ladder of participation" (see Figure 6.1) that sets out different levels of participation of young people (and adults) in different situations. Widely used in many contexts, this model is helpful in clarifying our thinking on student participation in the life of schools.

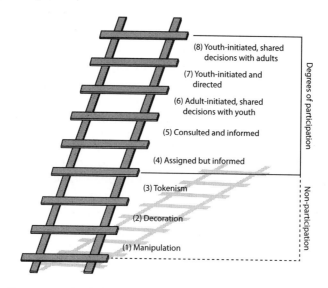

Figure 6.1: The ladder of participation (after Hart, R. (1992))

On this ladder, the bottom three rungs do not involve participation of young people at all. It is the upper five rungs that constitute participation, with the involvement of adults to varying extents.

In **manipulation** adults use young people to support causes and pretend that the causes are inspired by them (for example, very young children carrying placards with no understanding of what they say or mean). **Decoration** is when young people are used by adults to support a cause in a relatively indirect way, although without pretending that the cause is inspired by them (for example, children brought onstage to gather around someone making a speech on a topic that concerns young people). **Tokenism** is when young people appear to be given a voice, but have little or no choice about what they do or how they participate and their views are not taken seriously.

Hart recognized four levels of participation.

Level (4) Assigned but informed

Adults design the project with a designated role for young people. Young people understand the project and their role, and volunteer to take part. Their views are respected. *Example*: Students volunteer to take part in a charity event organized by teachers.

Level (5) Consulted and informed

Young people give advice on projects or programmes designed and run by adults. They are informed about how their input will be used and their views are taken into account in decisions made by adults. *Example*: Students contribute views and input to school committees of adults, who make the decisions. Students give their views on school publications being put together by adults.

Level (6) Adult-initiated, shared decisions with youth

Although adults initiate, young people are involved in all subsequent stages. *Example*: Students are full members of decision-making groups set up by teachers.

Level (7) Youth-initiated and directed

Adults are involved only in a supportive role. *Example*: Student-initiated club, society or activity, with a teacher as mentor.

Level (8) Youth-initiated, shared decisions with adults

Young people start and implement projects, coming to adults for support and input, learning from their life experience and expertise. *Example*: Students initiate an event but enlist teachers and other adults to share in the organization—with everyone sharing in decisions.

(Developed from a number of sources including McCreary Centre Society.)

Genuine participation, in Hart's terms, occurs when children:
- understand the purpose of the project
- know who made the decisions about their involvement and why

- have a real rather than a "decorative" role
- volunteer for the project after it has been explained to them.

Participation can be valid and effective at all levels. Indeed, there are some who consider that the ladder model is unhelpful—and that the five levels 4–8 are all equally worthwhile, according to context (see Carnegie UK Trust (2008)). However, the ladder does prompt us to consider how students can be encouraged and enabled to participate to the greatest extent.

Note that Hart's "highest" level is not reserved for students working alone. He argues strongly that young people benefit particularly from working alongside adults as equals—level 8. Young people (and adults) learn from the experience, each bringing "the special energies and perceptions of their generations" (1992: 44).

Key questions

- ▶ How important is student participation in the life of the school? Do students have too much to do to be involved actively in the running of the school?
- ▶ How do students participate in the life of your school?
- ▶ What are the levels of participation?
- ▶ Are there opportunities for young people to initiate?
- ▶ If not, is this because of their age/ability/experience, or for other reasons?
- ▶ Are there ways you could offer students more opportunities to participate at Hart's levels 7 and 8?
- ▶ Can you think of examples of students in your school operating at levels 1, 2 or 3?
- ▶ Hart's terms for these levels are clearly disapproving. How do you feel about this?

Hart and others have noted that in some contexts girls and boys may participate to differing extents and in different ways, for cultural or social reasons.

- ▶ Do girls and boys participate in different ways in your school?

Rudduck (2006) distinguishes between consultation and participation. "Consultation is about talking with pupils about things that matter in the school." In contrast, "participation is about involving pupils in the school's work and development through a wider range of roles and responsibilities, and through membership of committees and working parties, focusing on real issues, events, problems and opportunities." She points out that consultation may be perceived as being associated with power structures and hierarchies, with students able to speak only when authorized to do so by teachers.

Student consultation, and taking on board what we hear, seems an essential requirement. This is the bottom line—but this does not mean it is universal and can be taken for granted. And where it is happening, it can always be done better. Consultation can also be conducted by students themselves.

Although there are other stricter definitions of participation, we shall be using Rudduck's broader understanding given earlier.

What are the benefits of participation to students and the school?

Increasing student participation may involve schools in considerable effort, but the real and immediate benefits to students and schools are well demonstrated by research evidence. Two major studies of international research have been undertaken recently (Halsey et al 2006; Davies et al 2006). They found evidence that student participation enhanced self-esteem and confidence, developed skills of communication and collaboration, and had a positive impact on students' sense of responsibility. There was evidence of beneficial impact on attendance, behaviour and academic achievement. Students in democratic schools were happier, and developed a greater sense of control and of their own ability to influence events and direct their own lives. They were also more likely to be active citizens in the wider community. Two cautionary notes emerged. Young people became disillusioned when involvement was considered tokenistic and had no impact; and the time required for participation and consultation did conflict with other priorities (Halsey et al 2006).

With the benefits of participation established, we turn now to look at practical ways we can set about increasing it.

Reflection

▶ What are the communities of which you yourself feel part?
▶ How do you participate in those communities?
▶ In what ways do you participate in your school?
▶ What affects or determines your level of participation in your school?
▶ In relation to community participation, what does your own experience contribute to your thinking on student participation in schools?

How do we set about increasing student participation?

Student participation in schools will partly reflect the culture in the society and the school's legislative context. In Denmark, for example, students are represented on school boards in equal numbers alongside teachers. In Denmark, Germany, The Netherlands and Sweden students participate in curriculum and pedagogic planning within schools and play a part in educational planning at the highest levels (Davies and Kirkpatrick 2000; Davies 2002). But whatever the context, there is some room for manoeuvre. We can become so conditioned by the parameters within which we work that we forget things can be different!

Johnson (2004b), reviewing the literature, considered the following to be important strategies for schools wishing to enhance student participation.

- Adopt a whole-school approach—and announce it publicly.
- Ensure all teachers have the necessary skills and methodologies to work with students in participatory capacities. Undertake systematic professional development.
- Ensure democratic structures—for staff and students.
- Listen to what students say. This includes working to remove barriers to listening, such as time constraints; emphasis on delivering the curriculum and on assessment; discounting students' challenging views; limiting the range of areas students can comment on; and challenging teachers' beliefs that students cannot or should not make a valid contribution.
- Engage school leaders and teachers in critical reflection, by challenging assumptions. (An external facilitator can help.)
- Recognize and celebrate the outcomes of partnership with students.

Research and best practice (as in the example below, based on an extensive case study in Johnson (2004b)) indicates that participation should:

- involve as many students as possible
- be concerned with things that matter to them
- run through all areas of the school, not be seen as a discrete activity
- take different forms according to the context and the young people involved.

CASE STUDY

Increasing student participation in a primary school

On her appointment as principal, Kaye Johnson developed a planned approach to increasing student participation. She worked with colleagues to increase their own participation in areas such as decision-making. Staff meetings included cooperative activities and modelled teaching methods that could be used with children.

Specific initiatives with students included allowing the small existing student council to dwindle while introducing new ways for more students to participate in the life of the school. Older students became "school ambassadors" to welcome visitors and show them around the school. All students showed the school to their parents at an Acquaintance Night, and reporting processes were developed to involve students. A Kid's Conference week placed students in new mixed age groups to work with different teachers on school values. This led to volunteer teachers and students observing the playground to assess the extent to which school values were shown. Classes devised their own ways of selecting students to participate in Values in Action groups, in which students could initiate changes they wished to see in the school.

Key questions

▶ On what matters are employees consulted in your school?
▶ How do teachers and other staff participate in decision-making in your school?
▶ Are there areas in which students and teachers or adults are involved in joint decision-making?
▶ What are the constraints on consultation and decision-making by staff and students?
▶ What changes could be made to increase staff participation, before or alongside increasing student participation?

How can students participate in school operations and decisions?

Table 6.1 gives examples of the many ways in which students can play meaningful roles in schools, relevant to development as active global citizens.

Student involvement	Student roles
Supporting peers/as peer helpers	**Peer tutors:** helping students with academic and social skills learning
	Buddies: helping younger or new students make transitions into a new school
	Guides: helping new students or people new to the community; showing visitors around the school
	Academic assistants: helping students set goals, consider options and plan actions; tutoring in academic areas; acting as readers for non-readers; reading for blind students
	Referral agents: helping peers get connected to appropriate specialists
	Peer counsellors: helping others sort out concerns, brainstorm ideas and provide practical help
	Conflict mediators: assisting others to resolve disputes
	Peer educators: assisting others in learning and using important health and social information
	Role models: helping others learn appropriate behaviours
Articulating their views and seeing through appropriate changes	**Members of school council**
	Members of working groups and task forces
	Researchers: observation of lessons; in-school self-evaluation
	Educational planners: on a curriculum unit
	Associate governors/board members
	Members of staff appointment panels
	Representatives on external forums and committees
Leadership	**Lead-learners:** as leaders of discussions
	Initiators or leaders of activities: mini-enterprises; community service; newspapers or blogs; sports; clubs and societies

Table 6.1 (Developed from Whitty and Wisby (2007: 20), incorporating material from Peer Resources)

Peer helping

Peer helping provides students with valuable experience while benefiting school operations. As activities can be relatively "low key", they may involve many students. These include those less likely to win elections or to be prepared to take part in situations with a higher profile or requiring greater responsibility. Encouraging students to serve as peer helpers in a variety of capacities expresses the school's trust in young people and can be an important contributor to school ethos.

CASE STUDY

ALLISON BEECROFT/HARRISON PUBLIC SCHOOL/TORONTO, ONTARIO, CANADA

Moving towards inclusion of all

This small elementary school has a diagnostic special needs kindergarten class for students with physical and cognitive challenges. These children give teachers the opportunity to experience those who are "different" and to build friendships based on respect, empathy and understanding. Their teacher, Cheryl Libman, together with Allison Beecroft, involved these students in an initiative that another colleague, Paula Brown, was very passionate about. Mrs Brown's students were concerned about themselves and other students who felt isolated and who appeared to be "outsiders" in the school yard at recess and lunchtimes. Ms Libman's special education class, Mrs Brown and Ms Beecroft, along with a small group of interested junior level students, developed an Inclusion Network to develop strategies to help those students in need and to contribute to providing positive solutions for conflict within the school. The three teachers divided the large group into three smaller sections. "Peacemakers" completed peer helping and mediation training over a period of weeks. In this way, students would strive to solve their own problems. "Playground leaders" were equipped with new playground equipment, which they would use to include younger students who had no one to play with at recess, while the "media group" was responsible for advertising the roles of these groups, fund-raising and promoting understanding of the students in the special needs kindergarten class. The Inclusion Network hosted a school assembly to bring attention to the issues of inclusion and bullying. Students created their own poems, skits, and a PowerPoint® presentation with music to address anti-bullying issues.

This was a constructive way for the special education population not only to feel included in the school community, but to become leaders. Later, group members decided to change the name to the Friendship Group, giving it a more inclusive title.

There is a very extensive literature in the area of "peer helping", and a wide variety of training programmes available to schools.

Involvement in staff appointments

Save the Children UK and the Scottish Alliance for Children's Rights (2007) outline various ways in which young people can be involved in the appointment of people who will work with them. They can provide input to the job description or indicate the qualities they would like the person to have. They can submit questions for adults to ask at interview, or, in some cases, form part of the interview panel themselves. Showing candidates around the school or meeting them informally gives young people opportunities to form views that they pass to the selection panel. For teaching posts, they can provide feedback after a lesson taught by each candidate.

Children in a Scottish primary school wrote a person specification for a new teacher that was sent to the candidates. This included "to be patient, up to date, and always to arrive on time"! They wrote to candidates inviting them to tour the school. Children had a discussion with candidates before their interviews, and provided feedback to the selection panel, which was taken into account in reaching the decision (Save the Children UK and the Scottish Alliance for Children's Rights 2007).

Working groups/task forces

These are set up with a specific brief, and for a limited time. Students who would not be, or would not wish to be, elected to a student council can make a contribution to a working group or task force in an area of interest (for example, recycling, sports provision). This therefore widens student participation. To avoid possible conflict with student council interests, working groups and task forces can relate to an overall student or school council as reporting groups. Following Hart's model, considerable benefit can be derived by having working groups or task forces on which students serve alongside adults.

Citizens' juries

The English Secondary Students Association (ESSA) has recently piloted the use of citizens' juries in schools, following Australia's first youth jury (Parra Youth Matters 2003) and work on adult citizens' juries in various countries. A jury composed of randomly selected students is set up to make recommendations on a specific issue that affects students. The jury collects information, and expert witnesses (from the school community or outside) provide evidence and answer questions. It then deliberates and produces an opinion and recommendations to decision-making groups. On the ESSA model, juries involve students only, and are responsible for providing a specific student perspective.

Random selection of jurors is important as any student can participate and, if held with reasonable frequency, considerable numbers will. This process contrasts with volunteering or elections. Although some jurors may lack enthusiasm, this of course mirrors adult juries in court.

Student councils

The National Association of Student Councils (NASC) in the USA and School Councils UK present strong cases for student councils at school or classroom level. Students develop skills such as peer mediation, listening to and making reasoned arguments, and handling themselves when their opinions differ from those of others. They deal with real issues of direct concern while working with others. In good student councils, students benefit individually and collectively, and the school does too. The NASC concludes: "Every secondary school should have a student council." While many schools do, they take different forms and vary in effectiveness. Some are operating right at the top of Hart's ladder while others are substantially tokenistic.

The UK citizenship initiative has led to several recent research projects on student councils. A project in London schools involved a full-time practitioner working to develop student participation through student councils (Davies and Yamashita 2007). The study confirmed that school councils can be highly effective forms of student participation when six basic building blocks are present.

- A visibly committed head and senior management team
- Committed and skilled teachers to facilitate class/tutor group/ home room councils
- Clear lines of responsibility and job descriptions for school council work
- A full system of class/tutor group/home room/year/grade and executive councils, together with sub-councils, to involve as many students as possible
- Adult and equitable relationships in the school generally

- An action-oriented agenda for the school council, and one that deals with the core business of the school, which is teaching and learning

Emerging from their research, Inman and Burke (2002) recommend that councils should have the scope and power to debate major issues within the school and a formal consultative role in major policies and decisions. They should have a written constitution with frequent and regular scheduled meetings, held during lesson time. Meetings should follow best practice, with formal agendas and minutes. There should be clear and effective reporting mechanisms to students, teachers, board and parents, the direct involvement of senior management and formally structured involvement of other staff. They recommend that a council should have its own budget and a say in how money is spent more generally. They also advocated systematic training for staff and students.

With any form of student representation, effective communication between a council and its wider constituency is essential. The council needs to receive structured input and provide feedback. While a school council may be the focus for student participation, this can be extended much more widely. Davies and Yamashita (2007) reported enthusiastically on the extent of involvement of school councils in two schools in their study. Students on teaching and learning committees were trained to conduct systematic lesson observations and provide feedback to teachers on aspects such as interaction with students and styles of questioning. A behaviour panel undertook research on classroom disruption, mediated with specific problematic students and set targets for improved behaviour. Students gained new insight into their school, and teachers responded very positively to the initiatives.

While some primary schools find school councils effective, others take the view that such formalized structures do not work well for younger children, when consultations with the whole class may be more effective.

Children and staff at Preston Park Primary School, London, UK, undertook training to improve their school council, which had not been taken seriously. As a result, the organization and structure of meetings and feedback were improved. Councillors were assigned roles, time was allocated for reporting back, meetings were given a dedicated timetable space, and proposals were forwarded to governors and senior management. Attention was directed to those things the school could actually change, and successful initiatives included lunchtime peer mentoring and a healthy eating week (Moggach 2006).

At Wroxham School, a primary school in Potters Bar, UK, all children and staff participate in weekly mixed age circle groups, aged 4–11, led and minuted by students aged 10–11 in their final year. This ensures all students have a chance to participate, and the mix of ages is beneficial to social interactions within the school (Hertfordshire Grid for Learning).

Key questions

▶ How are students consulted about things that affect them in your school?

▶ On what areas are they consulted, and how are these decided?

▶ What part do students play in decision-making?

▶ What forms of representation do students have?

▶ Are the forms of student representation effective?

▶ How were they developed? How might they be changed?

▶ How could student ideas and opinions contribute more to decisions in your school?

▶ How could students and teachers or adults be involved in joint consultations and decision-making?

Student-led activities and initiatives

These provide important ways for students to contribute to school community life and develop and exemplify characteristics relevant to global citizens. In some cases, activities and initiatives may be directly related to global issues. Students may have opportunities to lead established clubs and societies, in the usual roles of chair, secretary, treasurer or committee member. There should also be scope for students to initiate new clubs and societies, as interests develop. Other opportunities for leadership include sports teams, service activities, and contributing to operations and organization of activities with adults (as in the International Global Citizen's Award, outlined in chapter 13). Individual students or groups may also initiate and lead specific initiatives.

Student participation in schools is important in its own right as it demonstrates, embodies and expresses our view of young people and their part in society. Students exercise rights, fulfill responsibilities and acquire experience that is important in other contexts. Participation can be particularly powerful when students are working alongside supportive adults and learning from them. But, while giving full attention to participation in our schools for global citizens, this is only the beginning. We should be encouraging our young people to participate in contexts outside school, and hoping they are beginning a practice and habit that extends and develops when they leave.

7 The global citizen teacher: Who we are and how we teach

Our young global citizens probably spend around one third of their lives asleep. On weekdays, they will spend up to half of the time they are awake in school, most of this in classrooms. If we are serious about working to create better global citizens, then what goes on in those classrooms is clearly very important. We can consider how that classroom experience can enhance the development of global citizens under four headings.

What we teach: the written curriculum—content—and our own modifications or interpretations of it

How we teach: our teaching methodology

Where we teach: the classroom or other learning environment

How we recognize change and development: recording and assessment

In educating global citizens, how we teach is at least as important as what we teach. So, we are considering it first. The other three aspects of the classroom experience are addressed in the following chapters. But before looking at how we teach, let us start with ourselves—the teachers.

Who we are

"Be the change that you want to see in the world."
Mohandas (Mahatma) Gandhi 1869–1948

If we are to work with young people to enable them to develop as better global citizens, it seems appropriate that we consider how well we show the features of global citizens ourselves. So, we begin with reflection.

Reflection

Look at your own definition, or your school's definition, of a global citizen.

▶ **To what extent do you show the characteristics of a global citizen as represented in your own definition?**

Look again at the definition of a global citizen given by Oxfam (see chapter 2). Consider each point in turn.

▶ **To what extent do *you* show these characteristics?**
▶ **Are you "outraged by social injustice"?**
▶ **If so, should you show this to your students in school?**

The Oxfam statement also expects community participation.

▶ **What is the nature of your own community participation?**
▶ **Is it at "a range of levels, from the local to the global", as Oxfam expects?**
▶ **How does "international education" as described by the IB learner profile (IB 2006a) compare with "global citizenship" as described by Oxfam?**

Key questions

▶ **Are we role models as global citizens? Should we be?**
▶ **It is possible to be a good teacher of singing without being a good singer. Can we educate students for global citizenship without being a good global citizen?**

What are we teaching for?

By this we mean what is our teaching directed towards? In our teaching for global citizenship, what importance do we attach to knowledge and awareness; to values and attitudes—caring about, empathy and compassion; and to preparing and enabling students to take action.

Educating *for* global citizenship, with its constellation of characteristics, is not the same as teaching *about* global issues. We can teach about global issues using the head only. But "global issues" are not a subject discipline with a body of knowledge and distinctive methodology to acquire. Rather, they are an assemblage of facts, opinions and ideas involving many disciplines. There seems no real purpose in teaching about them purely factually as an end in itself. The justification for teaching global issues as part of the curriculum is because of their importance to all our lives. They are "issues" because people care and argue about them, and, on our model of a global citizen, are motivated to take action. We cannot engage with them fully if we consider them solely as topics for intellectual study. They need to be approached with a global citizenship teaching methodology. We need to use the heart and hands as well as the head.

In teaching relating to global issues, students should therefore be encouraged to understand that:

- it is important to try to get to a working knowledge base—"the basic facts"—even though these may be disputed and changing, and this needs to be recognized too
- it is equally important to acquire knowledge and to keep abreast of developments
- our opinions should stem from a sound knowledge base
- different people can take different views from the same factual basis
- the issues have implications for our everyday lives—that is why they are global
- global issues raise ethical issues, which may have implications for our political views and our everyday behaviour.

This leads us into the area of pedagogy—how we approach educating young global citizens—head, heart and hands.

Reflect on what has been said so far about global teaching or educating for global citizenship.

▶ **What sort of teaching approach seems appropriate?**
▶ **How does this compare with the approach you use in your own teaching?**
▶ **To what extent are you engaged with head, heart and hands in this teaching?**

How we teach

The research evidence

There has been a recent upsurge of interest in citizenship education in various parts of the world, and in research into what makes it effective. The Citizenship Education Research Strategy Group undertook an extensive review of international research evidence (Deakin Crick et al 2004, 2005). The conclusion, directly relevant to global citizenship, was that "citizenship pedagogy ... will have at its core communication, facilitating and enabling, dialogue and discussion, encouragement to engage with learning, and relating learning to experience. This more conversational and negotiated style of teaching and learning involves mutually respectful teacher–student relationships where traditional authoritarian patterns of control are no longer appropriate." (Deakin Crick et al 2005.) They also concluded that teaching in this way may lead to improved academic attainment as well as to beneficial affective outcomes. There are implications. Teachers may need support to move from "traditional" teaching methods and content to learner-centred teaching and curriculums that relate to the students' experience. Power also needs to shift in the classroom, and many teachers may need to "let go of control" and pay more attention to the views of students.

In another recent study specifically on global citizenship, Lynn Davies and colleagues investigated perspectives of UK students and teachers (Davies et al 2004). Students wanted to find out about the wider world, had concerns about human rights and justice and wanted more political education. They particularly enjoyed interactive teaching methods and leading their own learning. They recognized that teachers were concerned not to scare or upset them, and were wary of expressing their own opinions. However, they "wanted uncomfortable information, and wanted to know what teachers thought".

Teachers recognized students' interests in real issues, but were wary of teaching about controversial issues for fear of being considered to be indoctrinating students. They lacked confidence to teach current controversial issues, and had received little or no training in this area. Students and teachers commented on feeling constrained by the National Curriculum, which may resonate with people in some other contexts.

Among the reactions of teachers to educating for global citizenship, some of which emerged in these and other research studies, are the following.

- I don't know enough about global issues to teach them.
- I don't know how I can teach for global citizenship.

- I'm apprehensive about teaching controversial issues.
- I don't have the time—to prepare, or in my course.
- I'm doing all of this already.

Let us look at each of these in turn.

I don't know enough about global issues to teach them

The solution to this lies in part in the statement itself. It assumes a model of teacher as subject expert transmitting knowledge to students. Although we obviously need some basic background knowledge, our expertise comes not from the knowledge base, but from our ability to acquire information, distinguish good sources from bad, reliable from unreliable, and information from opinion or wilful manipulation of facts. Working alongside students to research global issues is a powerful way for them to acquire skills and learn from our true expertise as more experienced learners.

We often talk of how important it is for students to "learn how to learn". Finding out about global issues does seem to provide a rich opportunity for students genuinely to do this, as we show them how to learn. While it seems essential for external curriculums to embrace global issues, it is to be hoped that they do not become yet another area of knowledge for teachers and subsequently students to acquire.

I don't know how I can teach for global citizenship

The Global Education Network of Young Europeans (GLEN) summarizes the pedagogy of global education, directly transferable to education for global citizenship. It is:

- learner-centred
- participatory
- partnership-based: the educator is not a teacher who transmits knowledge and skills, but is a learner her/himself
- concerned with addressing—in the learning process—reflection (head), emotions (heart) and activity (hand)
- experience-based
- activating
- empowering.

We need to shift from more traditional teaching methods to ones based on conversations and dialogue—from what Skidmore calls "pedagogic dialogue" to "dialogic pedagogy" (Table 7.1).

From pedagogic dialogue ⟶	to dialogic pedagogy
Controlled by teacher	Shared control between teachers and students
Directed towards "right" answers	Directed towards exploring possibilities
Right answers are valued	"Wrong" answers and risk-taking are valued
Closed teacher questioning	Open-ended speculative teacher questioning
Teacher has more "talk time" than students	Students have more "talk time" than teachers
Limited participation	Inclusive participation
Outcome-focused	Unpredictable
Teacher owns the truth	Truth is the shared outcome

Table 7.1 (Based on Skidmore (2002), as cited in Myhill (2007))

Dialogic teaching was practised by Socrates in ancient Greece. Teacher and student share a joint inquiry in the search for an outcome that is not predetermined, and at the start is unknown to both parties. According to one of its key proponents, Robin Alexander (2008: 25), dialogic teaching is:

- "collective—teachers and students address learning tasks together, whether as a group or a class

- reciprocal—teachers and students listen to each other, share ideas and consider alternative viewpoints

- supportive—students express their views freely, without fear of embarrassment over "wrong" answers; they help each other to reach common understandings

- cumulative—teachers and students build on their own and each other's ideas and develop them into coherent lines of thinking and inquiry

- purposeful—teachers plan and steer classroom talk with specific educational goals in view."

Alexander argues that on the basis of international research evidence "discussion and dialogue are the rarest yet also the most cognitively potent elements in the basic repertoire of classroom talk" (Alexander 2008: 31).

Cooperative learning, while beneficial in many purely academic contexts, is particularly appropriate in educating for global citizens and there is a substantial body of research on its effectiveness. For a succinct introduction see Johnson and Johnson (1996). More generally, participatory, interactive teaching is likely to use a wide variety of techniques, including the following.

Answering questions	Problem solving
Class discussion	Pair discussion
Group discussion	Group work of other kinds, including project work
Visiting speakers	Brainstorming
Reading	Asking questions
Online research	Research from books
Practical work	Undertaking experiments
Reflecting—orally, and in writing	Simulation exercises
Writing reports	Role-play activities
Debates	

Such teaching draws on the cultural diversity of the classroom and community. Although in teaching for global citizenship there may be a focus on discourse and discussion, critical thinking and reflection and problem solving are at its heart.

In considering our work with students as global citizens in all areas inside and outside the classroom, the notion of "accompaniment" is helpful. This emphasizes working alongside and providing support as we accompany them on their journey. The global citizen teacher's role is providing accompaniment not answers.

Reflection

▶ What are your reactions to this teaching approach?
▶ Is this how you teach already? Is your teaching very different?
▶ What do you see as the advantages of this approach?
▶ What reservations would you have about this pedagogical approach?
▶ If you wanted to incorporate more of this approach, how would you set about doing so?

I'm apprehensive about teaching controversial issues

"Too often we project the idea that all good people are on one side of a given issue; it follows that people on the other side are either bad or ignorant."

Nel Noddings (2005: 59)

"The reverse side also has a reverse side."

Japanese proverb

In addressing many global issues with students, we are likely to encounter controversy. Controversial issues are those that arouse strong feelings and/or deal with questions of values or beliefs and cannot be settled by facts. Claire and Holden (2007) elaborate. A controversial issue is one in which:

- the subject/area is of topical interest
- there are conflicting values and opinions
- there are conflicting priorities and material interests
- emotions may become strongly aroused
- the subject/area is complex.

Oulton and colleagues (2004) point out that different groups may be using different information, or interpreting the same information differently. This means that some controversial issues can be resolved as more information becomes available. However, differences in opinion may reflect different world views, sometimes underpinned by different values.

Working with students to enable them to handle controversial issues seems an essential part of what we should be doing in school. Listening to the views of others, responding to issues without becoming personal, and analysing issues critically are acquired skills. School seems the appropriate place for young people to acquire and practise them.

Some issues may be controversial to some people or in certain contexts only. It is helpful to identify issues as potentially controversial in advance so that one can be prepared. Just as students need to acquire skills to handle controversial issues, so teachers need to have the skills to help them to do so. There is an emerging consensus on what constitutes good practice in teaching controversial issues.

Dean and Joldoshalieva (2007) describe working with trainee teachers in Pakistan on teaching controversial issues—a context where they are not often addressed in schools. They developed four approaches:

- discussion—with preparation, management (by a teacher or student), summary and evaluation
- debate
- role play
- demystification.

Role play encourages students to see things from another point of view but to retain some detachment.

Demystification is a four-step process to analyse arguments put forward by others. It forms the basis of teacher training on handling controversial issues in Alberta (Clarke 2007).

- **Step one:** What is the issue about?
- **Step two:** What are the arguments?
- **Step three:** What is assumed?
- **Step four:** How are the arguments manipulated?

This process represents a dispassionate way for students to analyse and respond to the arguments of others in writing, on television, or in the classroom. And, of course, this approach can also be used as a mirror in which to analyse our own arguments.

But controversial issues lend themselves to discussions, when particular considerations apply.

1. Establish ground rules

Within the classroom, it is advisable to establish some ground rules—all sound common sense, when they are pointed out.

- Only one person talking at a time—no interrupting
- Show respect for the views of others
- Challenge ideas not people
- Use appropriate language—for example, no racist or sexist comments; no abusive language
- Ask everyone to express his or her view to ensure that everyone is heard and respected
- Students should give reasons why they have a particular view

These come from *Teaching Controversial Issues* by Oxfam GB (2006b), a short pamphlet with many helpful ideas and suggestions on the topic. (See also Holden 2007b.)

2. Consider your own role as teacher

Doug Harwood (1997) recognized six distinct roles that teachers may assume in different contexts when dealing with controversial issues (Table 7.2).

Teacher's role	Explanation	Observations
Committed	Teacher expresses and propagates own views	Can lead to a biased discussion Needs care
Objective or academic	Transmits an explanation of all possible viewpoints without stating own position	Students can be frustrated that the teacher does not give his or her views
Devil's advocate	Adopts provocative stances irrespective of personal viewpoint	This ensures all views are covered and challenged if a consensus develops early on; also helps to challenge students' existing beliefs
Advocate	Teacher ensures all viewpoints are represented, then presents personal viewpoint with reasons	Can make the point that it is important to consider all views before coming to one's own opinion
Impartial chairperson	Teacher ensures all viewpoints are represented; facilitates discussion but does not express personal opinion	Students can be frustrated by teacher not being prepared to share personal viewpoint
Declared interest	Teacher declares own viewpoint at the outset, so that students can judge later bias, then presents all positions as objectively as possible	Presenting the teacher's views first may lead students to give them undue attention.

Table 7.2

Teachers can adopt different roles at different times, even within a single lesson. But awareness of the role one is adopting seems important.

Some suggest that teachers should "stick to the facts". But "facts" can be contestable and our selection of facts is subjective. In any case, many issues are controversial because of feelings, attitudes and values, and failing to engage with these does not do justice to the nature of some issues.

Others argue that teachers should remain neutral in all discussions. However, as mentioned, research tells us that students like to know what we think (Davies et al 2004). For some students, the teacher may be the only adult they know (rather than see on television) who is prepared to share their views with them.

Hamashita (2006) suggests drawing on legal concepts. Teachers should ensure teaching does not "misrepresent" facts or opinions or mislead or "deceive" students. Information presented should not be false or unsubstantiated. It should not be presented as firm "facts" when it is in dispute. We also need to consider the effects of what we teach on our students. Could it cause hatred or harm?

3. Teaching strategies

Oulton and colleagues (2004) present further practical research-based advice on handling controversial issues.

- Acknowledge that balance is impossible to achieve in our teaching, and therefore make students aware of how to detect bias for themselves.

- Avoid strategies that encourage students to make up their minds prematurely. Rather, encourage open-mindedness, a desire to acquire more information and willingness to change one's mind.

- Use strategies that encourage students to recognize, respect and value the notion that a person's stance on an issue will be affected by their world view.

- Emphasize the importance of critical reflection, and recognize that prejudice comes from lack of critical reflection.

There is no necessary reason why teachers should act as facilitators in discussions, and encouraging and preparing students to chair discussions can be a powerful way for them to develop useful skills as well as their understanding of controversial issues. Donna Hurst and colleagues at the International School of Bangkok have developed a comprehensive methodology for older students (16 +) to lead and take part in discussions. This is available online at http://communitytheme.ibo.org/eng/post/students-facilitators-discussions.

▶ Are there any controversial issues being considered by teachers about aspects of your school?

▶ Could any of the methodology and advice available be helpful to you and your colleagues in handling these?

CASE STUDY

TAMARA BRAUNSTEIN/WEST AFRICAN COLLEGE OF THE ATLANTIC/SENEGAL

Controversial issues in the English classroom

IB English A2 is studied at near native proficiency level and options include global issues with a focus on Anglophone societies. In a recent semester, the teacher structured the global issues element around the Universal Declaration of Human Rights. As a liberal New Yorker teaching in predominantly Muslim Senegal, the teacher found it fascinating that countries reached consensus on such a large scale. The class discussed what should constitute a basic human right, and how can so many different countries/cultures agree on this? They talked about love and marriage, of interest to teenagers anywhere. Wide-ranging discussions considered free and arranged marriages, bride burning and dowry death.

The class established that, on the whole, people should be free to follow their hearts. As the issue of homosexuality would be dealt with in *The Color Purple*, the teacher asked about people loving others of the same sex and whether or not homosexuals should be entitled to marry—a topical issue in the USA. The Muslim students were appalled, as homosexuality is quite simply considered to be against nature. The teacher, without voicing her own opinion, played devil's advocate; the class did establish that maybe homosexuals should not be denied a right that is extended to others. Students suggested that perhaps "such people" could be housed in separate areas so as not to offend "decent" people. "Oh," responded the teacher. "You mean like *segregation*?"

The teacher's role in all this was to make the class think about the complexity of issues facing the world today and the Herculean nature of any attempt to get countries to agree on fundamentals. As a rule, the teacher never voiced her own opinion, but for any stated point of view would make the argument for its opposite, or encourage others in the class to do so. It was about making people think, at least enough to recognize that there are invariably two sides to any argument.

Consider each of Harwood's roles for a teacher in handling controversial issues.

▶ **Are there any roles you feel you should not take, or feel uncomfortable taking?**

Reflection

▶ **How do you feel about giving your own views in discussions with students?**

▶ **If you are prepared to do so, do you have any view of when in a discussion this should be?**

▶ **Should you only give your views when asked by students, or should you offer them whether or not your opinion is asked?**

▶ **If you do not feel you should give your views, what is your response to students who ask you for your opinions?**

I don't have the time—to prepare, or in my course

This is a genuine concern, and there are no easy answers. At primary and lower secondary level, increasing numbers of relevant teaching materials are available online (see "Teaching materials and resources" in chapter 9). For upper secondary work, commitment and ingenuity are required to incorporate global citizenship elements into classes under syllabus and exam pressure. Some suggestions for short and easily prepared activities come later in this chapter, and there are further ideas in chapter 8.

I'm doing all of this already

If this is really the case, then please give this book to someone who might find it more useful. But is it worth getting a second opinion from a trusted colleague? Or from your students?

The global citizen teacher

Let us return now to ourselves as teachers. What characteristics and attributes might we expect our teacher of global citizens/global citizen teacher to show? In a research review on how good citizenship (not specifically global citizenship) can be fostered, Gearon (2003) concluded that teachers should:

- aim for consistency in reinforcing the school's fundamental values
- reflect on their own values and the appropriateness of the example they set through their personal and professional conduct
- ensure that the learning that occurs through their relationships with their pupils through peer interactions and through the life of the school is as positive as possible
- reflect on the potential within school subjects and cross-curricular themes to raise questions of value

- help pupils to develop a sense of their own moral identity and to become gradually more aware of the complex and controversial nature of many moral values.

These are challenging expectations, particularly for those more used to dealing with matters of fact or technical expertise. The last two points may represent a particular challenge. Sharing perspectives between colleagues is likely to be very beneficial here, as some subject areas have traditionally been more concerned with "questions of value" than others.

In *Global Teacher, Global Learner* (1988), Pike and Selby list the characteristics of a "global teacher". More recently, Lesley Snowball (2007) sets standards for an effective "international teacher" and the Canadian project ACT! (Active Citizens Today) describes a "global educator". Pulling this work together and adding my own thoughts, a global citizen teacher:

- is interested in important and complex issues and concerns
- recognizes local, national and global dimensions in important issues
- brings a global perspective to the classroom and school
- embraces and welcomes diversity
- acknowledges and values multiple perspectives, values and attitudes
- is open-minded and willing to learn from the experiences of others in the classroom and beyond
- knows his or her rights and responsibilities as a global citizen
- addresses injustices and inequities within and outside the school
- makes the curriculum relevant and connected to the students' lives and concerns
- teaches students how to think and act critically
- models democratic ideals in the classroom by shifting the focus of decision-making from the teacher to the students
- employs a range of teaching and learning styles in the classroom to suit individual student needs
- promotes independent learning in others
- sets his or her work in context, and works collaboratively with others inside the school and in the wider community
- is actively learning and seen to be so
- says what he or she believes and believes what he or she says
- is a facilitator

- believes in human potential
- believes in the ability of the individual to make a difference, and encourages his or her students to believe and act accordingly
- is concerned with the development of the whole person
- is concerned with the future, and optimistic about it
- is prepared to show his or her humanity and fallibility in their work.

Producing a list like this is a great deal easier than living up to it! It is not intended to demoralize but to prompt reflection, and perhaps present an element of challenge. It is long, but each point is distinct and something would have been lost in reducing it.

Review the elements of the two lists.

▶ **How important do you consider they are as attributes of a good teacher of global citizens? You may like to group them in order of importance.**
▶ **To what extent do you show these characteristics?**
▶ **Which of these attributes do you find most challenging?**

Some of these characteristics are concerned with our qualities as people in general. How can we encourage students to care if we do not show care and compassion ourselves? How can we do this appropriately and professionally? (See, for example, Noddings (1992)) Some are concerned with personal engagement and action. Do we need to model it? This idea of our personal lives leading quite so directly into the classroom may be contentious. Some are specifically concerned with our teaching skills and attributes. Perhaps these are both the most relevant and the easiest to develop.

A final characteristic of the global teacher is humility. Global issues have become problems because of human action and decisions—actions and decisions of adults rather than young people. Perhaps we as the older generations should acknowledge this, and reflect it in our approach.

Sara Coumantarakis (1999), a Canadian worker on global education, reminds us of the underlying purpose of our work. "A global educator teaches toward a vision of the world in which the environment is cared for; human development is sustainable; human rights are protected; cultural diversity is valued and a culture of peace is the norm."

A conflict of pedagogies?

A distinct pedagogy is emerging from research in citizenship education and from practice in global, development and citizenship education. This is substantially different from "traditional" pedagogy directed towards subject-based acquisition of knowledge and skills and the attributes external examinations can reliably assess. A wholesale switch of pedagogies may not be possible or desirable: teaching critical thinking and problem solving lies at the heart of good teaching, whatever the label. But educating for global citizenship, with its emphasis on attitudes, values and action may well call for some adjustment. Here are a few suggestions for those grappling with introducing global citizenship into their teaching.

The "awareness, caring about, action"/"head, heart, hands" sequence of global citizenship is mirrored in the "three whats" sequence (see also chapter 12).

What?	Concerned with information
So what?	Concerned with its implications
Now what?	Concerned with future responses and action

Pedagogical approaches in addressing these three questions are somewhat different.

What?	Calls for acquiring knowledge and information and critical thinking, all in the context of possible controversy
So what?	Invites reflection and is more overtly concerned with values
Now what?	Calls for problem solving, imagination and planning to consider action in response

One practical approach is to break up teaching concerning global issues into sections along these lines, with different emphases and pedagogy to match. More generally, switch pedagogy when addressing global citizenship specifically. Short activities can be introduced in lessons that may adopt a different approach from the prevailing pedagogy.

Here are just a few thoughts about how to make some impact without taking too much time out from other work.

- Set aside 15 minutes a week for students to discuss between themselves, in pairs, an item in the news that relates to your subject but has relevance to global issues. Get the students to find the items themselves from television, newspaper or from the internet.

- Spend time in a lesson researching with students a topic that they choose relating to a global issue of relevance to your subject. Consider "So what?" and "Now what?" questions.

- Incorporate deliberate asides—brief comments that indicate a connection to a global issue or an aspect of global citizenship— without going into any depth.

- Display materials relevant to global citizenship in your classroom, even if they are not directly related to your subject. This indicates to students that you are interested in and concerned with these issues, and takes no time out of class.

- Be prepared for "teachable moments"—those unplanned opportunities that can arise when an excursion into global citizenship is appropriate. They can be used for private reflection, paired discussion, explanation of the factual background to a topic, or for students to record their thoughts in a journal.

- Include "moral moments". Research highlights the desirability of addressing ethical questions, or issues of value, in the subject classroom. Small-scale deliberate interventions to address ethical issues in "normal" teaching have been shown to have impact on students' ethical awareness (Clarkeburn 2002; Downie and Clarkeburn 2005). These interventions introduce opportunities for structured discussion in small interactive groups, when key topics with ethical implications are being taught.

Professional development

A number of development organizations have professional development resources available online to download (for example, Oxfam and WWF). Here are two online professional development programmes available and relevant to all.

Australia's **Global Education Project** has a 15-hour course introducing teachers to the concept and teaching of global education. Visit the website at http://www.globaleducation.edna.edu.au/globalperspective/index.html.

TeachGlobal at http://www.teachandlearn.net/teachglobal offers free training developed by the UK Open University and the BBC World Service Trust.

An increasing number of universities are offering options in global citizenship education, for example, Bath, Bath Spa, York in the UK; Montclair State University in the USA.

Individual teachers wishing to try out new pedagogy may like to become involved with the International Global Citizen's Award (see chapter 13). Undertaking in-school professional development with colleagues is also very productive, and necessary, if a school is committed to global citizenship education. This book might be a starting point.

To conclude our consideration of the global citizen teacher, here are a few thoughts from some experienced practitioners, giving their key tips on what to do—or not to do!

Merry Merryfield (2004), one of the leading figures in global education in the USA, recommends the following strategies in the classroom, and at school-wide level.

- Teach against stereotypes, exotica and the simplification of other cultures and issues facing the planet.
- Foster the habit of examining multiple perspectives and primary sources relating to people of minority cultures, or those whose views are rarely heard in mainstream texts or media.
- Teach about power, discrimination, conflict and injustice and their effects on the construction of knowledge, the use of language and people's world views.
- Provide students with cross-cultural experiential learning—opportunities to work with people from different backgrounds to their own.

Penney Clark (2000), a Canadian social studies specialist, emphasizes the importance of hope, an ethic of care and an orientation towards the future (Table 7.3).

	Our response
Hope	Ensure that in working with young people we do not "immobilize them with despair". Include positive initiatives and examples.
An ethic of care	"If students do not learn to care, the rest is for naught."
	Caring needs to be considered and reasoned, and to take into account all sides of an issue—not to be a diffuse and immediate emotional response.
Future orientation	Students need to be encouraged to learn from the past and the present, but look forward to the future.

Table 7.3

And finally, encouraging words from Desmond Tutu: "Do your little bit of good where you are; it's those little bits of good put together that overwhelm the world."

▶ **What aspects of your teaching would you like to develop to equip you better for educating global citizens?**

▶ **How can you set about doing this?**

Consider two lessons that you are due to teach within the next three days.

▶ **What simple and achievable changes could you make to these to give more attention to educating for global citizenship?**

▶ **Are there any changes in your personal life that you would like to make to enable you to be a better global citizen (teacher)?**

8 What we teach

"It is more difficult to change a curriculum than to move a graveyard."
Alec Peterson, first director general, International Baccalaureate
Organization, quoted in David Sutcliffe (2006)

This section considers how teachers and schools can adapt what they teach to reflect greater attention to developing global citizenship, particularly while working within external curriculum frameworks.

You may find it helpful to undertake an audit of current practice before reading this chapter (see the section on school-wide audits and benchmarks for global citizenship in chapter 3).

To modify what we teach to incorporate global issues and address global citizenship we can do the following.

- **Add** a curriculum component specifically dealing with these issues
- **Select, substitute or modify** an existing element of the curriculum
- **Permeate or infuse**
  - one or more existing subjects, or
  - the entire written curriculum
- **Introduce a new curriculum** that addresses global issues and the development of global citizenship more effectively

Adding a curriculum component

The addition of an element to the existing curriculum has some clear appeal. It addresses global issues overtly and everyone can see that a change has been made. Teacher and students can focus solely on the matter in hand, and the teacher can be a specialist in the area, or be prepared to become one. We can add a special course or a project, for example.

A special course

A number of schools have developed or are developing a course based on, or incorporating, global issues and global citizenship elements, and have added it to what students study.

CASE STUDY

A Global Affairs course

The school runs a weekly course called "Global Affairs". The main objectives are for students to develop an awareness of world events, to learn basic debating skills, to explore and learn to live with ideological differences, and to be able to view the media critically. The course is mandatory for IB Diploma Programme students and is entirely student-led. A typical session will include local and international news items, selected and read by students, and a debate on one of the issues covered, chaired and facilitated by students.

Student leaders, selected rigorously, schedule newsreaders each week, chair debates, update an information window on a regular basis and encourage their peers to prepare for the following debate. They will usually have some experience of debates from Model United Nations and similar activities. A teacher runs them through the basics of chairing debates initially, and gives them feedback after each session. If necessary, the school schedules a debate arranged by a teacher to provide a further model. It is important to have a teacher facilitating or observing regularly—otherwise, there is little possibility of genuine improvement through critical feedback and the whole thing can turn into anarchy.

Finding an hour a week to do this is in itself a challenge. The school set aside time for Global Affairs when it introduced the IB Diploma Programme. Other ways to find a slot include using lunch break, making it into an after-school activity or bringing students out of lessons on a rotational basis to minimize lost study time.

It is important that Global Affairs is seen as central to the curriculum, rather than an add-on subject, so teachers address global issues in other subjects too, for example, famous 20th-century speeches in the IB language A (first language) programme.

Setting aside an hour or so a week with enthusiastic volunteer teachers has some advantages and benefits. Finding that hour and those teachers may be easier than encouraging all teachers to introduce global elements. With a fairly open brief, teachers can be innovative in pedagogy and take on board students' interests and preferences without the usual pressures of external syllabuses and assessments. Such teaching can have considerable impact on students and the innovative practice of enthusiasts may be infectious within a school.

But unless they are part of more comprehensive curriculum adaptation, stand-alone courses may make global issues seem peripheral or discrete. There are resource and timetable implications too. Putting a course of this type in the lunch break or after school does nothing to dispel notions that it is peripheral. The one-hour model may be an effective part of a school's more comprehensive programme to educate for global citizenship. However, as Conrad Hughes notes above, it is not satisfactory as a school's only response.

A research project

Global issues lend themselves to a project approach with students pursuing their own interests individually or in small groups. It is possible to be experimental in pedagogy in a project even if it is more difficult to effect wholesale pedagogical change. An effective approach to project work in global citizenship, including research and practical action, and geared to students aged 11–16 is described in *Get Global!* (Price 2003).

Selecting, substituting or modifying an existing curriculum component

Social studies courses are obvious targets for modification and Thornton (2005) considers this in the US context. Offering a course within the existing timetable framework may be more practicable than finding time for something extra.

CASE STUDY

JAKARTA INTERNATIONAL SCHOOL/INDONESIA

Global studies

The school offers a course on global studies as part of its regular curriculum. It is a one-year credit course taught in year 10, and with no prerequisites. The course introduces basic terms and concepts from several social studies disciplines, supported by specific case studies drawn from around the world. Examples include child labour in the Indian subcontinent, development of the European Union, apartheid and reconciliation in South Africa, and global crises such as AIDS, environmental hazards and poverty. Emphasizing the importance of participation in change, the course challenges students to become involved in an ongoing community service project in their community. Information technology in the "global village" is closely examined, leading the student to understand and evaluate information media. The class debates the "pros" and "cons" of globalization. Building upon active skills such as problem solving and decision-making, the course is student-centred, focusing on an understanding of what it means to be a global citizen.

(Based on information supplied by Jakarta International School, Indonesia.)

Courses in personal, social and health education or citizenship can be modified by the school or educational authority, or both, to incorporate elements of global citizenship. Such programmes often have a different pedagogy and approach from subject teaching, and aspects of global citizenship fit in comfortably. Many of the excellent teaching activities devised by development organizations can be used here.

The Ontario Civics course (for year 10 students, aged 14–15) has included "Citizenship within the global context" as a requirement since 1999. Students analyse contemporary crises or issues of international importance, become familiar with rights and responsibilities within the global context, research individuals and NGOs that have had a global impact, and arrive at their own definition of "global citizen". Teachers are able to give greater additional emphasis to global citizenship and, in one classroom, students introduced a global dimension to their required civic action projects (Schweisfurth 2006).

Key questions

▶ **How do you address citizenship/personal/social/health education in your school?**

▶ **Is there scope to incorporate educating for global citizenship within this?**

▶ **Would this be by an addition to, or a re-orientation of the existing programme?**

The rest of this section concerns externally determined curriculums. What students actually study is determined at three levels.

- **External authority/curriculum body**—subjects, syllabuses and course elements offered to schools or required to be taught
- **School**—subjects, courses or elements selected by schools to offer to students
- **Student**—what the student selects from what is offered by the school

Subjects offered to schools by curriculum/examination boards

Table 8.1 gives examples of some less "traditional" courses for students aged 14–18, devised to address global issues specifically, or adopting a more global approach to a subject.

Curriculum/examination board	Course
Advanced Placement (1)	Environmental science
GCSE (2)	Environmental science
Cambridge International Examinations (CIE) IGCSE (3)	Development studies Environmental management Global perspectives (pilot subject)
IB Diploma Programme	Environmental systems and societies (standard level) World religions (standard level—pilot exam May 2009) Peace and conflict studies (standard level—school-based syllabus) Human rights (standard level—school-based syllabus)

(1) US College Board Advanced Placement (AP) exams (taken by high school and college students intending to enter universities)

(2) General Certificate of Secondary Education for students aged 14–16, studied in England, Wales and Northern Ireland

(3) International version of GCSE

Table 8.1

A brief consideration of some of these gives an indication of the range of courses available.

CIE IGCSE Development studies (syllabus 0453) focuses on issues that are particularly relevant to economically less developed countries. The syllabus covers poverty and development; industrial development, trade and globalization; population and development; and environment and development.

CIE IGCSE Environmental management (syllabus 0680) is concerned with education for sustainable development and is multidisciplinary. Four key topics are considered: natural resources; development of the environment; environmental impact; and environmental management.

CIE IGCSE Global perspectives (syllabus 0457) aims to develop students as "*active* global citizens" (CIE's italics). It encourages international and cross-cultural perspectives as students research issues, form a personal view and evaluate possible courses of action. Assessment includes an individual research portfolio and a group project. Areas of study are widely drawn, from "Law and Criminality" to "Conflict and Peace" and "Disease and Health". It remains to be seen how this interesting and innovative course is received and taken up by schools.

IB Diploma Programme World religions (pilot) encourages students to consider alternative world views—another important aspect of global citizenship. A selection of major world religions are studied, some in outline and others in greater depth, and students complete a personal investigative study (IB 2006b).

IB Diploma Programme Environmental systems and societies (standard level) is a transdisciplinary subject combining the knowledge and methodology of experimental sciences and humanities. Drawing on economic, historical, cultural, socio-political and scientific sources, it focuses on the relationships between societies and their environments, providing a holistic perspective on environmental issues. Students are encouraged to develop their own views, while recognizing the views of others, and their cultural bases (IB 2008a).

Subjects selected by schools and students

There is a considerable disparity between what is on offer to schools from external authorities, and what is actually taken up by them, as highlighted by Clayton Lewis (2006). Table 8.2 shows figures for 2007 entrants in selected subjects for Advanced Placement (AP) examinations.

Subject	% of schools offering the subject	Number of students	As % of total students	% increase on 2006 entries
US history	88	333,562	23	7
European history	36	91,040	6	7
World history	**27**	**101,975**	**7**	**21**
Environmental science	**20**	**52,416**	**4**	**17**
Human geography	**9**	**29,005**	**2**	**38**
Government and politics US	52	160,978	11	12
Government and politics Comparative	**8**	**13,358**	**1**	**5**
All AP subjects		1,464,254		Average 10%

Table 8.2 (Based on information from College Board (2007))

Within the entire range of AP subjects, world history, human geography, environmental science and comparative government and politics (in bold) have the most evident global perspective. Yet they are taken by relatively low numbers of students—no more than 14% in total, and in a relatively low proportion of schools. But encouragingly, recent growth rates for three of these subjects are the highest of all AP subjects.

In the IB Diploma Programme, environmental systems and societies (to be examined for the first time in 2010) combines elements of an innovative pilot subject (ecosystems and societies) with those of the increasingly popular but still relatively small environmental systems. This is a welcome move by the IB. The new course potentially impacts on more students than ecosystems and societies would ever have done.

The other IB subjects in Table 8.1 are pilots or school-based syllabuses, with small entries. School-based syllabuses are those devised by IB World Schools themselves. A student may include one school-based syllabus among the six subjects chosen. Such syllabuses are an important potential source of curriculum innovation within IB World Schools, some having evolved into regular subjects. One school-based syllabus is peace and conflict studies, devised by the United World College of the Atlantic over 30 years ago.

CASE STUDY

Lodewijk van Oord/United World College of the Atlantic/Wales

Peace and conflict studies

Peace and conflict studies (PACS) was first offered in 1977. Both the school and the International Baccalaureate (IB) were enthusiastic about the first experiences and the subject's potential for growth. It took almost 30 years, however, before other IB World Schools decided to offer the course to their students as well. Currently, peace and conflict studies is offered as a course in a handful of schools, with more schools on the way.

PACS provides an opportunity to explore issues of peace, violence and conflict at various levels of society, from the personal to the global. The course is underpinned by the assumption that conflict is not necessarily something to be avoided. Instead, conflict can be seen as a dynamic process, a "tool" for creating positive change wherever injustice exists. The course is interdisciplinary in nature. Students are encouraged to learn through activities and project-based experiences, and to evaluate their findings in group discussions and debates.

One of these activities is an individual writing assignment called "Facing my own prejudice". After considering the theoretical background to prejudice, each student identifies a group against which they hold a prejudice. They analyse this prejudice in class using theoretical studies. Students are given guiding questions: When did you first become aware of your prejudice? How often are you in direct contact with members of this group? Does this contact confirm or challenge your prejudice? Would you like to change it? If so, how could you do this?

The variety of prejudices students identify is always extensive. They openly describe their attitudes, and associate the group they dislike with often familiar stereotypes. It becomes more interesting when students start analysing the causes of their prejudice. A Norwegian student attributes his prejudice against Pakistanis to conformity: he realizes there is a general tendency in his social environment to think negatively about people from the Indian subcontinent. A Palestinian student bases her prejudice against Jordanians on one negative experience with a Jordanian soldier at a border crossing. The influence of friends, parents and the media are all factors that are brought forward as causes of prejudice in students' personal lives. In the final section of the assignment, students reflect on what might change their prejudice.

The reflective process students go through during the "Facing my own prejudice" assignment is typical of the course as a whole, and student feedback shows that students value this subject immensely.

Further reading: Van Oord (2006, 2008). The PACS subject guide may be obtained by contacting Atlanic College or the IB Curriculum and Assessment Centre.

Even within the "mainstream" regular subjects of the IB Diploma Programme, uptake by schools of subjects that might better enhance global citizenship is limited. IB geography, like many modern geography courses, includes much on global issues. Yet uptake is relatively low (less than 5% of Diploma Programme entrants (IB 2007c). This reflects both relatively low uptake by IB World Schools globally (geography is not an established subject in some traditions), and by students within those schools that offer it.

History is one of the most popular IB Diploma Programme subjects, with 29% of all students studying it at higher level. Although all students study core world history, at higher level students also select a regional option. Table 8.3 shows options studied by the 23,387 higher level history entrants in May 2007.

Higher level regional option	Percentage of higher level history entrants taking option
Africa	0.6
Americas	63.8
Europe	33.3
Asia/Middle East	0.7
Asia/Oceania	1.6

Table 8.3 (IB 2007c)

Most IB World Schools offer one regional option, and these percentages closely reflect the location of schools offering the IB history course, and the nationalities of students. A separate Islamic history subject attracted a total of 112 entrants at both higher and standard levels. Clearly, potential opportunities within the IB curriculum for schools and students to extend their knowledge of other countries by the choice of subjects or subject options within mainstream subjects are not extensively taken up.

Responsibility for selecting from the menu offered by external authorities rests with schools, which seem to be selecting conservatively. In some cases, higher education or national requirements or traditions influence the choice. But external authorities can nudge along adoption by schools of syllabuses that move them into new territory. The IB's history syllabuses have always required engagement with world history, and a new IB history higher level syllabus (to be examined from 2010) combines European and Islamic history. By combining popular European and less popular Islamic history, the IB may encourage more schools to stray outside the familiar. But schools still have to choose to offer the course, and students to select it.

Key questions

▶ To what extent are global issues addressed in current teaching in your school?
▶ In which subjects and subject areas are global elements more prominent?
▶ Is the approach to global issues geared to raising "awareness" only, or is the aim to get students "caring about" the issues and taking action? Is the approach educating for global citizenship?

> ▶ In which areas are global elements prominent or missing?
> ▶ If you offer externally assessed courses, what subjects do you offer that have an international or global orientation?
> ▶ What scope is there to encourage or require students to engage with global issues and global citizenship through the subjects you offer?

Other course elements

Some programmes require particular elements in addition to subject courses. For example, all IB Diploma Programme students write a research-based extended essay, which normally falls within one of the subjects of the IB curriculum. The next case study describes an interdisciplinary extended essay in world studies—a modification of the normal requirements—introduced by Mahindra United World College of India (UWC) four years ago and now being piloted more widely.

CASE STUDY

Cyrus Vakil/Mahindra United World College of India/India

IB extended essay in world studies

World studies extended essays (WSEEs) choose a *global* problem or concern and make a close *local* investigation of it in one or two studies. Essays usually begin by demonstrating the global scale of an issue, proceed to a solid "body" on the case study/studies, and end by reconnecting the local issue to the global one. Students are encouraged to offer public policy pointers, at least for the local context, in their conclusion.

Since analysis of problems, policy measures and their evaluation is almost always interdisciplinary, so is the WSEE. Students are encouraged to be "problem-centred" and "solution-centred" in their approach, not bound by conventional disciplinary boxes. An essay on infant malnutrition in a rural community in Southern China may, for example, borrow methods from the biological and health sciences (measurement of the body mass index) and the social sciences (designing questionnaires on diet, collecting and analysing quantitative and qualitative data).

The best essays involve substantial hands-on fieldwork, and students require some preparation by the school—local language learning, data collection and analysis, and some awareness of the strengths and limitations of various social science research methodologies.

Where some students have tripped up in recent years include: taking on a study that is too large or diffuse; drawing conclusions that overstate the case, asserting that the issue can now be tackled effectively universally by employing the same means that proved successful locally; or taking on a subject where, lacking the direct means of collecting data, they must necessarily rely on government, UN or NGO reporting.

WSEEs have demonstrated that 17-year-olds have the intellectual and emotional maturity to maintain the critical, yet objective, stance towards their subjects required by such explorations. For many it has been the most rewarding learning experience of their two-year diploma and no less than 55% of Mahindra UWC students now do the world studies extended essay.

Modification or substitution of an existing element of the curriculum is more practicable in many contexts than a new additional element, with fewer time and resource implications. However, in contrast to the Mahindra experience, such initiatives may have limited uptake. Students will not necessarily select some of the courses offered, whatever their quality. In examination courses, choice may be constrained by higher education considerations, or selecting subjects that support one another. However, as part of a battery of measures for schools to address global citizenship, modification or substitution of existing courses and elements certainly has its place.

Modification of a component or course taken by *all* students gets over the uptake issue. In this regard, the new Cambridge Pre-U is interesting. This is a curriculum and qualification developed by Cambridge International Examinations (CIE) for the last two years of school prior to university. Teaching began in September 2008. A required component of the Pre-U is a component *Global perspectives and independent research (GPIR)* with the global perspectives element taught over the first of the two years. GPIR is also available as a stand-alone qualification for students wishing to take it alongside GCE A levels.

The CIE Pre-U global perspectives course involves the study of a number of topics of global significance using a four-stage "critical path", as illustrated in Figure 8.1.

Deconstruction		Detailed analysis of a point of view
Reconstruction		Identification and evaluation of evidence for and against competing points of view
Reflection		How have the student's own views been affected by the inquiry?
Presentation		An opportunity to address an issue holistically and in detail

Figure 8.1

Assessment includes a substantial essay and a multimedia presentation. Inclusion of a compulsory global issues-related element in an academic programme for the upper secondary level is a significant step.

Schools for global citizens should certainly be considering introducing new courses or programmes specifically to address global citizenship, and looking carefully at the subjects and syllabuses they choose to select from those offered by external authorities. But if a school is committed to educating for global citizenship, something must be done about other subjects, and, ideally, about the curriculum as a whole. One way is to modify the existing curriculum in various ways, and the other is to introduce a new curriculum. For reasons that will become obvious, we will consider the second option first.

Introducing a new curriculum

This is a major undertaking with considerable implications across the whole school or section involved. Two strategies are available.

- Devise a new curriculum within the school
- Introduce an existing curriculum, already developed and available

Relatively few schools can devise their own curriculum from scratch. For those that can, this book will provide some suggestions. More schools are in the position of considering the introduction of an alternative off-the-shelf curriculum for a section or for the whole school. Of course, a complete curriculum is about far more than global citizenship and global or international dimensions. Nevertheless, there are two comprehensive, well-established and widely adopted curriculums that specifically address international or global dimensions throughout. These are briefly described below.

The International Primary Curriculum (IPC) (2007) is offered in over 500 schools in more than 50 countries. It "provides the support teachers and schools need to help primary and elementary children learn as twenty-first-century international citizens" and "focuses on academic and personal development, and the development of global awareness". "Learning Goals" include some goals that are specifically intended to help young children develop national and international perspectives, such as developing awareness and understanding of the independence and inter-dependence between peoples and between countries, and of the similarities between peoples and countries. The IPC Early Years Programme (for children aged 4–5) includes an "international aspect", and written units include "coverage of international goals". In the IPC Main Programme (for children aged 6–12) units of work include a number with a specific international slant, such as "What Price Progress?", "What Does Our World Look Like?" and "The Global Swap Shop".

The International Baccalaureate (IB) offers three distinct programmes for the full school age range: the Primary Years Programme for students aged 3–12, the Middle Years Programme for students aged 11–16, and the academically challenging IB Diploma Programme for students aged 16–19.

In November 2008, there were 2,425 IB World Schools in 131 countries, and an estimated 665,000 students engaged in IB programmes. The IB encourages the development of "international-mindedness" in all activities, described and defined in the IB learner profile. All IB World Schools must commit to working towards meeting a number of programme standards and practices, elaborated by a series of practices and used in regular self-study. Standard A2, for example, is: "The school promotes international-mindedness on the part of the adults and the students in the school community" (IB 2005).

The IB Primary Years Programme (PYP) curriculum is organized around six transdisciplinary themes that include significant international/global elements. For example, the theme "How we organize ourselves" includes the interconnectedness of human-made systems and communities; the structure and function of organizations; societal decision-making; and economic activities and their impact on human-kind and the environment (IB 2007a).

The two following case studies illustrate how intercultural and global issues can be addressed within "units of inquiry" in the Primary Years Programme.

CASE STUDY

ABHIMANYU DAS GUPTA/PATHWAYS WORLD SCHOOL/GURGAON, INDIA

A tale of two cities

The school has developed a unit of inquiry "A tale of two cities", which takes shared humanity as its underlying theme. Although the unit visits two different cities in the same country, it is aimed at making students realize that even within a country, especially one as vast and diverse as India, there exist cultural differences. The students inquired into the food, clothing, arts, language and historical monuments of two distinct cities of India, and also interacted with the people from these cities. The cities were New Delhi, with a more cosmopolitan yet typically North Indian flavour, and Hyderabad, with a unique blend of traditional Islamic influences and a hi-tech yet typically South Indian ethos. At the end of the unit, students realized that human emotions are the common thread binding together a melee of cultures that are moulded and defined over centuries due to a variety of circumstantial factors. The experience opened the minds of the Indian students and also the non-resident Indian children, who were confused about their roots, as well as the expatriate kids.

CASE STUDY

IRENE DAVY AND TANYA LOW/SUNNYBROOK SCHOOL/TORONTO, CANADA

Penguins and polar bears

The school has defined the concepts it feels are central to a global education. Teachers incorporate them throughout the programme and teach them explicitly in the units of inquiry. "Penguins and polar bears" is a year 4 unit about the polar regions, under the transdisciplinary theme "Organizing the planet". Students focus on the global concepts of stewardship, sovereignty, conflict, responsibility and environment. The central idea of the unit is: *The geography of the polar regions creates unique stewardship and environmental challenges.*

Global issues guide the unit throughout. Newspaper clippings are used to identify issues and generate discussion, as well as to drive student inquiry. An article about sovereignty in the Canadian Arctic being challenged by Russians was the springboard for inquiry about the melting icepack, global warming, national boundaries and the importance of resources. Using these current events, which are relevant to the students, provides powerful opportunities to explore the related concepts.

Students had great fun with an analysis of Coca-Cola® adverts, which showed penguins and polar bears meeting. A discussion about responsibility and the role of the media, resulted in interesting observations, such as, "They're teaching me the wrong things just to try and make money."

An article about tourism in the Antarctic provided the gateway to exploration of the ecosystem, tourism and questions of sovereignty. Especially fruitful were the discussions about shared global responsibility for this part of the world and its vulnerability due to the lack of a national government.

International Polar Year (2008–9), a scientific project with 60 nations working together to raise awareness of polar issues, provided a rich resource for teaching action. Students created a campaign to promote understanding of the unique nature of the polar regions and the need for collective action to preserve these environments.

By incorporating current events, this inquiry has grown from a knowledge-based geography and habitat unit to a truly transdisciplinary one addressing global issues at primary level.

One of the students expressed it eloquently in her reflection: "The polar regions are important places to our world because they store most of our water and there are lots of special animals. I think all of the nations need to take stewardship over the land."

The **IB Middle Years Programme (MYP)** emphasizes intercultural awareness, "the notion that school communities should encourage and promote international-mindedness by engaging with and exploring other cultures" (IB 2008b). The "areas of interaction" of the MYP include environments, human ingenuity, and community and service, all of which relate to global citizenship.

In the **IB Diploma Programme**, guides to each subject include a section on international dimensions. The reference to global issues and the extent to which assessment addresses global dimensions varies considerably between subjects. For example, language A1 (first language) includes a study of world literature in translation (IB 1999). Language A2 (for students with an already high level of competence in the language) includes a global issues option (IB 2002a). Language B (second language) includes cultural awareness as a required component (IB 2002b). Economics includes a significant emphasis on development economics (IB 2003), while business and management embraces cultural perspectives, the nature and significance of change in local, regional and global contexts, and the social and ethical responsibilities associated with businesses operating in international markets (IB 2007b). Science syllabuses have been amended to incorporate greater reference to global, ethical, social and environmental issues, and teachers' notes give further guidance in these areas. IB Diploma Programme students engage in service as part of the creativity, action, service (CAS) requirement.

A recent IB initiative is the introduction of a three-year IB community theme: sharing our humanity. This aims to engage members of the whole IB community—parents, employees, students and teachers—with certain key global issues. Schools are encouraged to share existing work in this area, and to engage further with the theme in all areas of their work both in and outside the classroom. The IB is addressing the theme in conferences, in its magazine *IB World,* and through a dedicated web platform (http://communitytheme.ibo.org). While there has been strong interest and support for this voluntary initiative, some have argued that the IB should be strengthening global issues in the mandatory curriculum.

CASE STUDY

QING LIU, LOUISE DAVIS, DIANE HOLLOWAY/BEIJING CITY INTERNATIONAL SCHOOL/CHINA

Global dimensions in the middle years classroom

Qing Liu introduced poverty and educational opportunities into her teaching of Chinese as a second language. In a unit "Earning pocket money" she discovered that her students had never earned money, but only ever spent it. She showed them a Chinese movie *On the Way to School* about the efforts of a 13-year-old girl in a poor village in China to earn the ¥24.8 ($2) necessary for her first-year fees in secondary school. The film had considerable impact on the students, who had taken money and education for granted. "I never knew that ¥24.8 could mean that much! And it's so hard to earn!" Qing comments: "Students became more involved in projects at the school that aim to help disadvantaged children. I believe that relating a unit of work to a real global issue, and to children of the same age but from a different life situation, can be of great benefit and can influence future actions in a very positive way."

Louise Davis, also at Beijing City International School, used an ecological footprint calculator as the centrepiece of teaching geography as part of a year 9 unit "How can I be a responsible citizen?" The calculator asks detailed questions about all aspects of lifestyle relevant to students, but avoids them having to work out energy use at home. "The first unit is always the geography of clothing. In this, they look at where their clothing comes from and the conditions under which it is produced. They consider issues such as logos and fair trade. They also play the simulation game from Christian Aid, Trading Trainers, developing empathy with Indonesian home workers who produce the sneakers the students all wear." Students choose the order of the subsequent units on water (connecting with science work), alternative energy sources and recycling, and food production. "Throughout it all, at the end of each unit, we go back to the carbon footprint calculator to see whether the classroom studies have made any impact on the lifestyle choices the students make and their carbon footprint. It is heartening to see the changes in these global citizens."

The calculator can be found at http://www.educ.uvic.ca/faculty/ mroth/438/environment/webstuff/footprint.html archived at http://www. webcitation.org/5aBUl6GAe.

Diane Holloway took her science class out into the community. In work on water "the class visited a local sewage treatment plant, a tap water museum, a park lake and a water canal. The students learned that Beijing had had two reservoirs but that one was now so polluted it was not longer useable." This was the catalyst stimulating them to think what action they could take to help ensure clean water supplies. "Action was the key word and this is where the students had the most difficulty. What to do? How do I do it? I provided the students with a list of reference sites: Ryan's Well, WaterAid, WWF, and Roots and Shoots." They found out more about the issue and groups made plans to raise funds—a disco, a basketball game, selling a reusable shopping bag—for a chosen charity project. "Students used the scientific method to lay out their action plans, stating a problem, making a hypothesis, creating a procedure, recording their results and analysing their plan's success. I assessed their work and wikis based on the programme criteria of one world, communication and scientific inquiry. The words of one of the student groups sum up the best possible outcome for the assignment: 'The global issue is the most serious problem in our modern world. Just our five people can't change the world. But somewhere, there have to be groups like ours. A small number of people can't do as much as a large number of people, but a large number of people was also a small number of people at the beginning.'"

Introducing the IPC or one or more of the IB programmes into a school is likely to result in considerable change, and can undoubtedly contribute to the development of an enhanced international or global dimension. But much is also down to the school. The *necessary* enhancement of international and global dimensions simply by adopting these curriculums is somewhat limited, and individual schools operating the IB programmes show very considerable variation in the extent to which they give attention to developing good global citizens. But the programmes enable and encourage schools to make a considerable shift towards doing this more effectively.

Permeating or infusing existing subjects or the whole curriculum

There are strong reasons for a thoroughgoing attempt to permeate and infuse the entire curriculum. Global issues can and should arise in many different subject and curriculum areas. Incorporating education for global citizenship in all aspects of the curriculum indicates the school's commitment and involves all teachers.

But individual teachers may be making efforts alone. Whether working individually or collectively, similar considerations apply. A syllabus or curriculum can be modified in order to promote the development of global citizenship by:

- including global issues wherever possible
- drawing examples and perspectives from diverse cultural, social, economic and national backgrounds
- addressing issues with a time and futures dimension
- stressing interconnections, interdependence and local–global dimensions
- valuing teaching that promotes the development of attributes of an active global citizen (see chapter 7).

You may find it useful at this point to revisit the brief outline of theoretical aspects of global education in "Educating for life in a global world" in chapter 1.

Permeating or infusing a curriculum to enhance development of global citizenship requires a clearly articulated framework. With the background of chapter 2 we can now take this further, drawing on work and practice in a number of countries.

The Canadian Global Education Network's *Global infusion: A guide to bringing the world to your classroom* (2005) highlights a number of student outcomes for global education, including that students will learn:

- to understand the connections between peoples, cultures and environments around the world
- to understand that all human beings have similar potential and aspirations but are not equally able to realize them
- to look at global issues from different perspectives.

The Curriculum Corporation's (2002 and 2007) *Global Perspectives: A statement of global education for Australian schools* identifies five "global education issues":

- globalization and interdependence
- identity and cultural diversity
- social justice and human rights
- peace-building and conflict
- sustainable futures.

The UK Department for Education and Skills (2005) set out eight "key concepts" that "provide a conceptual framework of thinking about and building (the global dimension) into the curriculum". These are:

- conflict resolution
- social justice
- values and perceptions
- sustainable development
- interdependence
- human rights
- diversity
- global citizenship.

In this context global citizenship is used rather narrowly, although it is recognized that it relates to and permeates the other key concepts.

Look also at Oxfam's "key elements", as set out in chapter 2. There are considerable similarities here, partly reflecting the influence of Oxfam on thinking in the UK and Australia, but also the convergence of views as different bodies consider our common challenges. The education for sustainable development programmes mentioned in chapter 2 are also relevant.

Both the Curriculum Corporation and DfES documents expand helpfully on the issues or concepts, essentially identifying student outcomes. Although these documents are devised for particular national contexts, much is of general interest and relevance. There is considerable overlap, but there are also some particularly helpful sections in each.

Drawing on many influences, Figure 8.2 is a simplified outline curriculum framework for an education for global citizenship. It gives a list of the global issues or topics in which awareness might be expected, at least in those who are older. The horizontal arrows direct us, through "caring about" certain concepts, to the right-hand side, away from knowledge towards action and involvement. Certain global issues are associated with the development of particular concepts, although there are considerable interactions. Running vertically are three other concepts that permeate all the work. The diagram reinforces the notion that awareness and knowledge are not enough, or not, in the end, important in themselves. Any curriculum for global citizenship must be taking students beyond knowledge to concern and caring; and beyond that to making a difference on the ground. Global citizenship should not become simply another subject to study.

People think in different ways. Oxfam (2006a) has elaborated a curriculum for global citizenship in more traditional form. This sets out the various elements of knowledge and understanding, skills and values and attitudes it considers should be developed at different ages, from early years (under 5) through to students aged 16–19. Table 8.4 shows extracts from this document. This is equally helpful in whole-school planning or for the individual teacher working out what it is appropriate to address with students in class. The challenges posed by this campaigning development NGO are very evident. To my knowledge this is the only published curriculum for global citizenship although schools may have their own. This, and the depth and extent of Oxfam's experience in education in this area, mean it is influential.

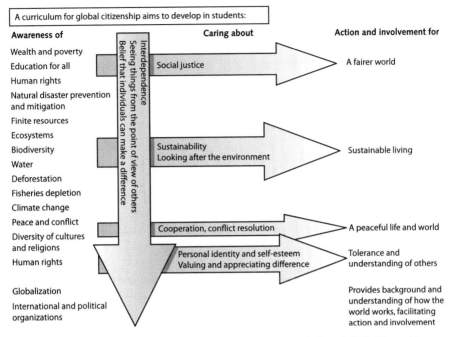

Figure 8.2: A simplified outline curriculum framework for global citizenship

Activity

You may wish to develop or identify, within your school, your own basic document setting out the knowledge, skills, values and attitudes that you are trying to develop while educating for global citizenship. Refer to the full Oxfam, Department for Education and Skills and Curriculum Corporation documents online. You may find one of these to your liking, or you may wish to develop your own.

To save time, it may be best to begin with one of the documents already available and refine and develop your own from this as you go along. If all your time and energy are spent planning, you won't have time for practical implementation—and for learning from the experience you gain from this.

Resist the temptation to focus on knowledge. Values, attitudes, skills and a capacity and motivation to take action and get involved are also essential.

		Early years: under 5s	Ages 5–7	Ages 7–11	Ages 11–14	Ages 14–16	Ages 16–19
Knowledge and understanding	Social justice and equity	What is fair and unfair / What is right and wrong	Awareness of rich and poor	Fairness between groups / Causes and effects of inequality	Inequalities within and between societies / Basic rights and responsibilities	Causes of poverty / Different views of the eradication of poverty / Role as global citizen	Understanding of global debates
	Sustainable development	Living things and their needs / How to take care of things / Sense of the future	Our impact on the environment / Awareness of the past and the future	Relationships between people and environment / Awareness of finite resources / Our potential to change things	Different views of economic and social development, locally and globally / Understanding the key concepts of possible and preferable futures	Global imperative of sustainable development / Lifestyles for a sustainable world	Understanding of key issues of Agenda 21 / Lifestyles for a sustainable world
	Ability to challenge injustice and inequalities	Beginning to identify unfairness and take appropriate action	Beginning to identify unfairness and take appropriate action	Recognizing and starting to challenge unfairness	Starting to challenge viewpoints that perpetuate inequality	Selecting appropriate action to take against inequality	Campaigning for a more just and equitable world
Skills	Cooperation and conflict resolution	Cooperating / Sharing / Starting to look at resolving arguments peacefully / Starting to participate	Tact and diplomacy / Involving/including society and others	Accepting and acting on group decisions / Compromising	Negotiation	Negotiation / Mediation	Negotiation / Conflict resolution
Values and attitudes	Empathy and sense of common humanity	Concern for others in immediate circle	Interest in and concern for others in wider sphere	Empathy towards others locally and globally	Compassion / Sensitivity to the needs and rights of others	Sense of common humanity and common needs	Sense of individual and collective responsibility
	Belief that people can make a difference	Willingness to admit to and learn from mistakes	Awareness that our actions have consequences / Willingness to cooperate and participate	Belief that things can be better and that individuals can make a difference	Willingness to take a stand on global issues	Willingness to work towards a more equitable future	Willingness to work towards a more equitable future

Table 8.4 (Extracts from "Curriculum for Global Citizenship" (Oxfam 2006a))

CASE STUDY

Curriculum mapping of global citizenship elements within the IB Diploma Programme

From 2003–5 St Clare's, Oxford reviewed the entire curriculum of its IB Diploma Programme students to address global citizenship more effectively across all areas. Teachers brainstormed the characteristics of a global citizen. IB teachers then devised their own outline curriculum for global citizenship in a series of professional development days. Keith Allen writes: "After developing our initial global citizenship curriculum, we wanted to evaluate how much we were doing already. Our aim was to facilitate the development of global citizens *within* current activities as fully as possible, rather than 'adding on' lots of components. So, we started to 'map' our practice on to our goals.

Goals	Components of IB Diploma Programme course											
Knowledge and understanding related to culture and beliefs	Lang. A1	Lang. B	Indivs. & socs.	Science	Math	Arts	TOK	EE	Per. soc. health ed	Int. days	Acts.	Res. exp.
Understand how accepted ways of behaving differ from one society to another												
Understand the daily realities of people less fortunate than themselves												

Key: Lang. A1 = first language; Lang. B = second language; Indivs. & socs. = individuals and societies (humanities); TOK = theory of knowledge; EE = extended essay; Per. soc. health ed. = personal, social and health education; Int. days = international days; Acts. = activities; Res. exp. = residential experience.

Shading indicates degree of coherence between goals and practice.
■ High ▓ Medium ▒ Lower ☐ Little or none

Figure 8.2: Mapping exercise

The main outcomes of this mapping exercise were threefold.

First, it identified relative contributions of different areas.

Second, it stimulated a number of departments to revise practice to promote our global citizenship goals more effectively. English A1 added Chinese fiction to world literature choices and arranged for people who had lived through the Cultural Revolution to visit classes. Language B teachers devised a common project called 'Uncrossing the wires'. Students researched how the media presented a common issue (initially, how world leaders are portrayed). Chemists included more micro-scale chemistry in practical work to reduce environmental impact. Activities staff amended their range of activities, including study visits to Northern Ireland. Residential staff led conflict resolution workshops in their regular 'house meetings'.

Third, it exposed the 'gaps' that we needed to address."

(Based on Allen (2004))

So, you have an overview of student outcomes, and the knowledge, skills, attitudes and values you wish to bring into the curriculum. You may have set out in a document your own articulation of these. Chapter 7 emphasized the importance of us as teachers and of our pedagogical approach. How do we bring all of this to bear in our work in the classroom?

Sara Coumantarakis offers the following checklist of things to consider when planning work in global education, or what we are calling education for global citizenship.

- Is the activity cooperative rather than competitive?
- Does it provide opportunities for taking further action?
- Does it connect global with local?
- Does it examine root causes?
- Does it examine the historical context of a situation?
- Does it examine power issues?
- Is it participatory and experiential and does it address various learning styles?
- Does it address the whole student (intellectual, social, psychological, spiritual) and connect with his or her experience?
- Does it include a futures orientation?

Here are some further points to consider when reviewing a lesson or unit of study to incorporate perspectives related to global citizenship.

- Are examples and case studies drawn from different international and cultural contexts?
- How can views and perspectives representing different national and cultural perspectives be presented and considered? Can they be presented in people's own words?

- Is it appropriate to seek out contributions relevant to the subject or lesson made by people from different countries and cultures and to draw on knowledge traditions other than the prevailing Western perspective, for example, views of indigenous people on care for the environment; contributions from Islamic and Chinese scholars to maths and science?
- Can I make use of artifacts and pictures from different national and cultural backgrounds?
- Are any representations of other cultures or countries stereotypes in any way?
- Can I include reference to one or more global issues?
- Am I focusing on problems? Can I focus instead on issues? Can I ensure solutions and ways forward are also considered?
- What underlying assumptions are there in what I am teaching? What can I do about this?
- How can I give students the opportunity to consider their own views on ways forward?
- Can I introduce ethical interventions, pointing out where ethical issues arise and providing opportunities for students to discuss them?
- Can we consider and demonstrate the relationship between issues at different levels, from the local to the global? Can we see that the global is in the local?
- Can we look at the interconnections between past, present and future?
- What opportunities are there to encourage students to research and think how others might take a different view, and why?
- Can I draw on cultural and international diversity in the students in my class?
- Can I provide opportunities for students to acquire experience of working with others of different national and cultural backgrounds
  - by pairing/grouping people of different backgrounds in the classroom
  - through classroom visitors (including colleagues and parents) with different backgrounds from students'
  - through electronic connections with others outside the classroom?

- Am I employing pedagogical techniques that explicitly seek to develop the skills and attributes of global citizens?

We are not always aware of our own preconceptions and biases. You may find it helpful to discuss a lesson or unit of study with a colleague as "critical friend".

Educating for global citizenship within subject studies

Below are a few suggestions as to how certain subject studies can incorporate educating for global citizenship. These draw on the UK Department for Education and Skills booklet *Developing the global dimension in the school curriculum* (2005), the Curriculum Corporation's *Global Perspectives: A statement of global education for Australian schools* (2007) and Pike and Selby's *Global Teacher, Global Learner* (1988).

First languages

- Studying stories, texts and media (fiction and non-fiction) from different countries, cultures and perspectives
- Selecting materials that address global issues, for example, poverty, conflict
- Providing opportunities for students to discuss global, ethical and controversial issues
- Consideration of global, social and political issues and their coverage in media in different countries
- Developing awareness of different perspectives; recognition of cultural stereotypes and bias in literature and media
- Drama to explore experience of others, for example, from different cultural or national backgrounds
- Factual writing on global issues
- Creative writing on relevant issues, for example, imagine a world without oil or wild places, or a country that tries to make itself self-sufficient
- Contact with native speakers from different cultural contexts

Other languages

- As for first languages, when students have sufficient proficiency
- Emphasis on relationship between language and culture
- Study of aspects of culture associated with the language
- Encouraging or requiring students to study a language from a very different cultural context

History

- Studying different regions through a thematic approach (world history)
- Examining sources representing different perspectives, for example, views of religious and ethnic minorities within a country; gender-based views. Examples: Arab perspective on the Crusades; Chinese perspective on the "Opium Wars"
- Addressing themes such as peace and conflict; imperialism and colonialism; slavery; trade, interdependence and exploitation; migration
- History of regions relevant to students in the school
- The historical importance of access to resources, for example, land, oil, water
- Appreciation of the connections between the past, present and future

Social studies

- Developing a personal sense of place and identity
- Knowledge of student's own country and culture and of the context in which they are living and studying
- Connections between people and places—from simple connections in primary school ("Where does our food come from?") to political and trade connections with older students
- Diversity of people, places, religions, languages and cultures
- Human rights and responsibilities, and their universality
- International organizations (UN and its agencies, NGOs, Intergovernmental Panel on Climate Change) and key agreements (United Nations Declaration of Human Rights, 1948; Convention on the Rights of the Child, 1989; Millennium Development Goals, 2000)
- Distribution of, access to and use of resources such as water, oil, fish, timber
- Population change and migration
- Study of individuals of note from different countries and cultures
- Globalization

Arguably, it is in social studies that the best, or at least the most obvious, opportunities for considering global and international dimensions arise. However, this seems no reason for efforts to address global citizenship to be confined solely to this area.

Science

- Basic human physical needs as an example of shared humanity. Consideration of uneven extents to which these basic needs are met, and reasons for this
- Humans and the environment; climate change; sustainability
- Earth's resources and their use; uneven distribution of and access to resources
- Energy, including pros and cons of fossil fuels, renewable energy, nuclear power
- Biodiversity and biological interdependence
- Global health issues: global infectious diseases and worldwide attempts to address them; diseases of poverty and affluence
- Science as an example of international cooperation—publications making science available widely
- Contributions to science from different cultures, and by people from different backgrounds, for example, Islamic contributions to astronomy and other areas of science
- International scientific projects, for example, human genome project, IPCC
- Importance of personal collaboration and cooperation in science practical work in school
- Data, case studies and examples drawn internationally
- Opportunities for discussions on the global implications of aspects of science; also of ethical issues arising
- Scientific theories and their formulation and acceptance in different cultural contexts; how political or other outlooks can slant scientific research or determine acceptability of scientific discoveries

Mathematics

- Mathematical notation, games and puzzles in different countries and cultures
- Contributions of people from different countries and cultures to development of mathematics, for example, the contribution of ancient Egyptians, Babylonians, Greeks, Arabs, Indians and Chinese to the development of algebra centuries before it was introduced into Europe; formulation of modern concept of zero by Indian mathematician Brahmagupta
- Universality of mathematics

- Examples drawn from global issues to develop and exercise mathematical skills, for example, human population growth as an example of exponential growth; calculating gradients of population growth curves to indicate growth rates; mathematical basis of life expectancy; use of extensive UN data in statistical studies
- Consideration of ethical implications of disparities revealed by mathematical approach to certain parameters of global significance

The arts

- Study of art, crafts, design, music from different cultures and traditions
- Cultural context of the arts, for example, Islamic design and non-representation of human form in recent centuries
- Methods and approaches to arts and crafts in different countries
- Musical instruments from different countries—studying and playing
- Different forms of musical notation
- Images and symbols in the arts related to culture
- Addressing global issues in the arts—taking a global issue as a subject for investigation and expression
- Impact of globalization on the arts

Health and physical education

- Physical activities and games from different countries and cultures; their relationship to different cultural traditions
- Consideration of basic human physical needs; inequitable access to basic resources and the implications of this for physical development
- Global health issues: importance of global infectious diseases; diseases of poverty and affluence; pandemics and epidemics; specific world health issues such as SARS, Avian flu and HIV/AIDS
- Importance of sports and games in cultural and political relations between countries
- Global sports events and festivals
- Ethical aspects of sports and games at international level, for example, use of growth enhancers
- International organizations and sports

- Globalization of sports, for example, universal rule book for football; implications of teams composed of different nationalities

Maths with a message

Students in Laos follow a national curriculum, and use standard textbooks. Here is a question that appeared in the book for year 4 maths:

"At a wedding party, 100 guests are invited knowing that each guest should drink 0.5 liters of beer (one bottle of beer is 0.65 litres). How many bottles of beer should be ordered, and how many crates? (One crate contains 12 bottles.)"

(Laos national grade 4 mathematics textbook, lesson number 60, page 164 (1997).)

Parents and teachers in one village were concerned about the reference to beer in a textbook for young children. They felt it sent out an unwelcome message. They decided to develop a version of the question that was no less challenging mathematically, but sent out another message—one of social responsibility:

"You want to buy a snack that costs 4,000 kip. If you have 21,000 kip, how many snacks can you buy? How much money will you have left to share with each member of your family?"

The next case study describes how global issues teaching within the curriculum led to student-initiated service to the local community.

CASE STUDY

PAUL HORKAN

Education for the poor

Students at the International School, Dhaka were studying a research unit called "Education for the poor" as part of a politics theme in the IB Middle Years Programme English A (first language) course. Students researched education and literacy rates in different contexts, including the host country, Bangladesh, and presented their findings and suggestions for action to their peers and teachers.

This inspired two students to initiate a weekend school programme for students from a local, poorly resourced school, initially in computing, and to subsequently develop and extend it as part of their community, action, service (CAS) requirement.

The student organizer Wasi Khan explains: "The whole purpose of the weekend school was to foster education among those who are disadvantaged ... It gave the children the opportunity to utilize some of the luxury we enjoyed in our school such as computer labs, fully equipped classrooms and a well-facilitated gym. The weekend school consisted of 40 students, 18 student volunteers and 5 different subjects. It also had its own code of conduct, uniform and curriculum. The responsibility that came along with it was also tremendous but also significantly improved my communication, organizational and managerial skills.

Just imagine if all the privileged schools around the world adopted such programmes. This would not only increase the efficiency of our educational infrastructure and resources but also make illiteracy history!"

Students naturally enlisted the help and support of teachers as necessary. Volunteers and participants were keen and eager to jump on board. It is still an annual event and is continually evolving and developing. This illustrates how a simple activity in the classroom can reach students, make them aware of global concerns and inspire them to take on a role and develop in so many aspects.

Activity

1. Look at the full Oxfam curriculum for global citizenship (in Oxfam 2006a). Consider how your curriculum could be adapted to address Oxfam elements.

2. If you are working from a written syllabus or curriculum determined by others, look at it again. Highlight any specific references to international and global issues.

   ▶ In what ways are you encouraged to address global issues in the syllabus?
   ▶ Is the focus on facts and information about global issues, or is the controversial and contentious nature of many issues recognized?
   ▶ Is there encouragement to address student attitudes and values in any consideration of global issues?

▶ What other aspects of international or global elements does the syllabus include?

▶ Can you identify immediate areas in which you could develop or enhance international and global dimensions within the syllabus?

3. If you are teaching for an external examination, sort out past papers for the previous two years.

Highlight any examples where international or global elements are addressed. Identify where international or global elements might have been addressed.

▶ If there are references to international and global elements in the syllabus, how are these reflected in the examination papers?

4. Consider the lessons you will be teaching next week.

Identify two lessons in which you could look to address international and global elements more overtly.

Refer back to the checklists on pages 112–114.

Consider how you can enhance the international and global dimensions in these two lessons.

▶ Are there ways in which you can give students greater opportunities to participate in the lessons?

▶ Can you give students opportunities to discuss matters relating to a global issue, as a class, in pairs or groups?

▶ Are there ethical issues inherent in what you will be covering in the lessons?

▶ Are there opportunities to encourage students to consider or take action relating to a global issue within either of these lessons?

Don't be too ambitious in what you propose to change. Try something that you feel confident about, but also something a little more challenging—even if it is only a small change.

After you have taught these lessons: review the lesson(s) with the amendments to enhance the global/international dimensions.

▶ How did you feel about the changes you incorporated?

▶ How were they received by students?

Reflect on what you have learned from the preparation and delivery of these lessons.

9 Where we teach and what we teach with

In this very practical chapter we are concerned with the classroom environment itself, and the resources and materials we use for learning within it. At their best, classrooms for global citizens are windows on the world, but also bring the world into the classroom.

Classroom layout

As we saw in chapter 7, educating for global citizenship often involves a pedagogy in which students are active and participatory with opportunities for cooperative learning. For this we need an enabling, not disabling, classroom layout. Obvious features of a classroom for global citizens are:

- chairs and tables set out to enable and encourage interaction and group work
- a physical organization to encourage independence and responsibility
- access to books and other relevant resources
- access to the internet for personal research within the classroom
- ample display space.

Activity

Review the layout of your classroom.
▶ Why is the layout the way it is?
▶ What teaching and learning activities does it suit?
▶ Are there teaching and learning activities you would like to do that the layout prevents or makes difficult?

Prepare an action plan for improving your classroom layout for educating for global citizenship.

Displays

Displays can indicate our commitment to global citizenship and make quick impact without undue effort. Vast sums are spent by advertisers putting images and messages before our eyes. Yet displays in secondary schools, in particular, are often sparse. In an age when people are used to soaking up what is around them, we are losing opportunities for students to learn. In even the most engaging lesson, the student mind can wander, as eyes gaze at the walls. A photo or quote can stimulate students to reflect in those gazing moments.

Through displays we can:

- convey information
- challenge preconceptions
- encourage reflection
- reflect diversity, including cultural, linguistic, ethnic and social diversity
- reinforce values
- convey messages
- make a statement
- get students thinking
- reflect diversity of viewpoints
- value students' work
- provide a more stimulating learning environment.

Maps embody assumptions. We can make these evident, or challenge them, by displaying maps using different projections. The Peters projection map represents land mass areas, and is often described as "corrective". "Upside down" maps (for example, MacArthur's map) place south at the top, with Australia prominent. The Worldmapper website offers nearly 600 printable maps in which the area of a country is related to a particular variable, such as number of working physicians, per capita debt or incidence of malaria.

Other examples of display material for classrooms for global citizens include the Millennium Development Goals (posters from Oxfam Education), the UN Universal Declaration of Human Rights (United Nations Publications), the UN Convention on the Rights of the Child (from country offices of UNICEF), *The Two Mules: A Fable for the Nations* (Society of Friends (Quaker) sources) and photographs of the earth seen from space.

There are some compelling snippets of information about global issues that have considerable impact. Quotes and sayings also have their place. Here are three on sustainability:

"The frog does not drink up the pond in which it lives."

Indian proverb

"Only when the last tree is cut, only when the last river is polluted, only when the last fish is caught, will they realize that you can't eat money."

Native American proverb

"Don't blow it—good planets are hard to find."

Quoted in Time magazine

And a lesson all young global citizens would do well to learn:

"Until the lions have their historians, tales of the hunt will always glorify the hunter."

Ewe-mina (Benin, Ghana, and Togo) proverb

Given the challenges facing young people in the years ahead, some motivational quotes may be in order—and perhaps not only from people who are over 50, or dead. Students can search out ones they like from people they admire.

Digital technology enables us to have changing visual displays or displays from internet sites—or perhaps world news. Anathema to those of us of a certain age, that's how young people seem to take in information. This might be something to consider for common areas, rather than the classroom.

Activity

Look at the displays in your classroom.

Try to see them from the perspective of a student; a parent.

▶ What messages are you sending by the displays—apart from the ones you intend?

If you have a colleague as a "critical friend", visit each other's classrooms and answer these questions for each other.

Teaching materials and resources

Vast and growing amounts of material on global issues are available. There are also some excellent resources for teachers, such as prepared lesson plans, games or simulations—often from NGOs. Teachers are still left with considerable challenges when considering their use in teaching. First, there is the time taken to research and find suitable resources. Second, there is the question of when and how to use them, given curricular constraints. Aware of these challenges, here is a deliberately short list of recommended websites directed at teachers.

The Association for Science Education (ASE) has a dedicated section on global dimensions in science teaching: visit http://www.ase.org.uk.

Facing the Future, a US organization concerned with global issues and sustainability, has some excellent online materials and books to purchase: visit http://www.facingthefuture.org.

Global Eye is a website of the UK's Royal Geographical Society. It has many teaching resources relating to global issues for all ages: visit http://www.globaleye.org.uk.

Oxfam Education (http://www.oxfam.org.uk/education) produces an excellent catalogue of printed materials (for teachers and students) and posters that can be ordered directly. The catalogue can be browsed online. It also produces teaching materials and short, very useful publications for teachers—available free online.

The United Nations and its agencies are good sources of data. The UN cyberschoolbus website (http://www.un.org/Pubs/CyberSchoolBus) is focused specifically on schools.

UNICEF (http://www.unicef.org) has a dedicated youth website **Voices of Youth** (http://www.unicef.org/voy). National committees also have resources for teachers (for example, http://www.unicef.org.uk/resources/index.asp).

WWF has teaching resources concerned with sustainability and the environment: visit http://www.wwflearning.org.uk/wwflearning-home.

The websites listed below give information on a range of resources and link to hundreds of websites on particular global issues and concerns.

Global Education, a website from AusAid (the Australian Agency for International Development), includes teaching materials and background information. Although designed for teaching in Australia, many materials are suitable for use elsewhere. You can search for lesson plans by age group and for background information on particular topics: visit http://www.globaleducation.edna.edu.au.

Global Dimension, set up by the UK Department for International Development, has a very useful and large searchable database of worldwide resources and links (books, posters, websites) in English only. Information is provided about all resources and links. Although some material relates to the UK, many resources are of more general interest: visit http://www.globaldimension.org.uk.

The website of **Global Education Centre** in New Zealand produces two online publications, *Global Issues* and *Global Bits*, each focusing on a particular issue. It has many useful links: visit http://www.globaled.org.nz.

Given the contentious nature of many global issues, selection of resources needs to be particularly careful. Sourcing resources internationally seems particularly appropriate. Here is a checklist for reviewing individual learning materials for global citizenship work.

- Does it include international and global references?
- Does it make any assumptions about different countries? Does it present one country or group of countries as in some way superior to others?
- Does it represent the interests of one country or group of countries? Or does it deal more even-handedly in its references to different countries and cultures?
- What terms does it use to describe groups of countries? For example, does it use the term "underdeveloped", or less emotive terms like "North" and "South"?
- Who are the authors? Where does the resource come from? Is there likely to be a particular slant because of the authors' backgrounds?
- Does it avoid bias in its consideration of issues? If it is taking one particular line, is this clear from the outset?
- Does it avoid racial, gender, age and other stereotypes?
- Is it inclusive in any images it includes? For example, are there images of people of both sexes, of different ages and of different ethnic groups?
- When describing complex issues, does it present different viewpoints? Are the different viewpoints from countries in different parts of the world?
- Does it talk of "issues" or "problems"? Does it include background to the issues and explain why, in some contexts, there are problems? Does it include indications of positive moves to address issues?
- Is it up to date?
- Where data is included, is it from reliable sources? Does it provide references for all data included?
- How is data used? Is it used to advance a particular set of views? Or is it used more impartially?

- Are complex matters oversimplified? Is there a suggestion that there are simple causes and easy solutions to complex issues?

In evaluating children's books for bias, there is a very useful and short article on the InTime website.

Reflection

> ▶ Is your teaching of global issues and addressing global citizenship limited by the resources you have?
>
> ▶ If so, is this because of time constraints, or financial resources, or for other reasons?
>
> ▶ If your teaching is not limited by access to resources, what are the factors constraining you?
>
> ▶ How can you move forward to give greater prominence to educating for global citizenship?

ICT-based projects

Modern technology enables students to communicate and collaborate with people in other countries and contexts and thereby to introduce a global dimension into work in all areas. Here are just a few schemes that enable schools and students to develop connections and collaborate on projects.

One of the best established is **iEARN**—the **International Education and Resource Network** of over 20,000 schools and youth organizations in more than 115 countries. The iEARN website hosts collaborative projects initiated by teachers and students in member schools—on global issues or making use of the global diversity of participants. Schools can join an existing project or, after some experience of using the website, initiate their own.

GLOBE (Global Learning and Observations to Benefit the Environment). Registered schools in participating countries undertake research investigations based on the environment and the Earth system, working with leading scientists as part of global projects. GLOBE student scientists collect and transmit data and receive reports on compiled data from all participating schools. Extensive supporting resource materials are available, and participants can take part in online forums.

Challenge 20/20—a programme of NAIS, the US National Association of Independent Schools—partners classes at any grade level from schools in the USA with counterpart classes in schools in other countries. Each team, with students from two or three partner schools, agrees a global issue on which it will work. All interaction is through technology, with no travel requirement. Visit http://www.nais.org and go to **Conferences & Programs**.

iNET (International Networking for Educational Transformation) hosts regular student online conferences on global issues. Discussions are based on materials students submit. Recent conference topics include "New technology: A threat or a promise?" and "Do you live in a 'global village'?"

Use of information and communication technology (ICT)

Whether accessed in class or at home, students need to develop the capacity to distinguish good from poor resources, and to detect the partisan. A few websites may be of help here.

Media Awareness Network, a Canadian not-for-profit organization concerned with media education, has a website with many useful resources that help develop media literacy.

A useful student handout "How to Detect Bias in the News" is available at http://www.media-awareness.ca/english/resources/educational/handouts/broadcast_news/bw_bias_in_the_news.cfm archived at http://www.webcitation.org/5YRwbyoLd.

The interactive website developed by the Ministry of Education, Singapore, teaches students (lower secondary) to detect bias in text: visit http://www3.moe.edu.sg/edsoftware/ir/files/soc-detecting-bias/index.html.

Global News uses online English language news services from around the globe as a key resource to help students develop critical thinking and questioning skills on the media and on key global issues: visit http://www.globalnews.org.uk.

Digital citizens

More generally, students need to become effective "digital citizens"—functioning responsibly and carefully in their interactions with and in the digital world. This is another aspect of global citizenship. Nine aspects of digital citizenship have been recognized, including online etiquette ("netiquette"), rights and responsibilities, health and wellness, and self-protection (Ribble). Education for digital citizenship is a developing field. See, for example, Ribble and Bailey, and Ribble and Bailey (2007).

A cautionary note on the use of ICT

While screens can truly provide students with "windows on the world", they can also screen young people from beneficial contacts and influences. Neuroscientist Susan Greenfield (2008) warns: "We could be raising a (generation who) are in distinct danger of detaching themselves from what the rest of us would consider the real world." Students also need to discover the global in the local among their fellow classmates and in the real world around them.

Windows on the world

Outside speakers can be an excellent way of bringing the world into the classroom. In some countries NGOs will provide speakers to visit schools. In other contexts it may be necessary to use personal contacts. The stories of individuals who have lived through conflict or experienced poverty can also be very affecting. New communication technology enables us to interact with people in real time, even when we are not in the same physical location, as the following case study describes.

CASE STUDY

Robert Ford/The Ridings High School/near Bristol, UK

International learning through videoconferencing

The school uses videoconferences (VCs) in many of its partnerships with schools and charities in 14 countries. The school sets up approximately 40 VCs a year. This enables students to interact with experts, or those with particular experiences in many parts of the world. The VC is like having a lesson or an interactive lecture. A VC is often backed up with online learning using a website offering a wiki for project resources and blogging for students and staff to communicate. A combined approach makes sure everything works well.

With the annual "Genocide" series of VCs, history and politics students link up with Eastchester High School, NY. In a different focus each week (The Holocaust, Rwanda, Cambodia, Bosnia and Darfur) a speaker (a survivor, NGO, academic expert) talks and takes questions. Students continue the dialogue afterwards. Often they will make a display for their peers and/or a presentation at the culminating conference. Participating in a VC is motivating for students, and not just for high-flyers.

Costs are falling all the time and expensive technology is not required. But a good ICT support person is very helpful. Once set up, competence improves through practice. In the school's VC work, teachers have collaborated with Mike Griffith of Global Leap, a specialist VC project. Visits between partner schools are beneficial, but not necessary. As Arthur C Clarke said, "it is about communication not commuting."

International learning within the curriculum is coordinated through an international department. Examples of how the school has used VCs include:

- ▶ English teachers working on myths and legends with year 7 students, linked with Schools 24 and 56 in Tomsk, Russia
- ▶ design and technology, and geography in a joint year 9 project on water in Africa with St Augustine's school in Gambia
- ▶ music and drama departments working with schools in Europe and Singapore on a project "Show me your music and dance".

Videoconferencing in a leading Chicago school is described in The Global Dimension: Walter Payton College Prep High School at http://www.edutopia.org/global-dimension-walter-payton.

- ▶ What aspects of global citizenship does the use of ICT facilitate or enable?
- ▶ Are there possible drawbacks of using ICT in educating for global citizenship?
- ▶ If so, how can these be addressed or overcome?

How we use resources

An important and easily changed aspect of life in the classroom is how we use resources—whether we use them with care and respect, or not. Here are a few ways in which we can model responsible global citizenship in our use of resources in the classroom.

- Use all resources and materials carefully.
- Use recycled paper. Use both sides. Re-use scrap paper.
- Be careful with the use of heating and lighting.
- Try to recycle unwanted or used resources.

Reflection

Consider the whole classroom experience for the young global citizens you teach—what they are taught, how you teach them, and the learning environment and resources.

▶ In what ways can you make changes to make their learning and development as global citizens more effective within your own classroom?

▶ Can you make these changes on your own initiative alone, or do you need to enlist other people, or obtain additional resources?

▶ How can you give greater attention to the development of key attitudes and values related to global citizenship in your teaching?

▶ How can students be involved in deciding what these are?

▶ What aspects of education for global citizenship are particularly well handled in a classroom context?

▶ What are the limitations of a classroom in school as the environment in which young global citizens are educated?

10 Visits, links and connections

Getting out of the classroom enables students to have first-hand experiences of the wider world and provides further opportunities for action as a global citizen. In this chapter we consider how global citizenship can be nurtured outside the school through visits and various activities, and through more extensive partnerships with schools in other countries. This leads into the next chapter, which looks specifically at activities in which students take action as global citizens inside and outside school.

Visits and excursions

Classroom-related visits to galleries and museums, national parks and places of environmental interest all have their place in educating for global citizenship. Visits can be arranged to recycling facilities, water treatment plants, power stations, farms, factories, zoos and many other places that help develop students' awareness of global issues and concerns. Students can become more familiar with other cultures and outlooks in visits to religious buildings, with the opportunity to talk to adherents of a particular faith, or to a school that teaches in another language. There is also scope for action during some visits. For example, a visit to a beach can include 15 minutes' beach clean-up. If coordinated with the appropriate authorities, a visit to a wood or forest can include tree planting or weeding of alien species.

There is no need to travel far to undertake effective activities with strong global relevance and significance—and, for some schools and students, longer trips are precluded by cost. Many local issues can be set in the context of global issues—relating local issues to the global, and considering the impact of global issues on local situations. As communities become ethnically and culturally more diverse, greater opportunities are available for students to meet people from differing backgrounds close to home. In local trips, ecological impact can be reduced by selecting transport carefully—perhaps with students being involved in the assessment of alternatives—and by reducing food waste and packaging.

The benefits and opportunities provided by local trips have become rather eclipsed in recent years by attractions of travel abroad, and some schools have an array of such trips for many purposes. Global travel has, perhaps a little too readily, been seen as a way in itself of promoting international understanding or global citizenship. Although overseas travel is more accessible, it is the quality and depth of the encounter and reflection rather than frequency or distance travelled that matters. As Marcel Proust comments: "The real voyage of discovery consists not in seeking new landscapes but in having new eyes."

Having said all this, a well-planned and executed visit abroad has the potential to provide a uniquely enriching and mind-shifting experience for students, simply unavailable in any other way and playing a significant part in their development as global citizens. Visits may be specifically concerned with the development of young people as global citizens (cultural visits, Model United Nations, Global Issues Network, service learning). Others may be less obviously so (concert or sports tours). More recently, and after the vogue for overseas trips became well established in some schools, the ecological downside of air travel has become apparent. Whatever the benefits of a visit involving air travel, it now seems apparent that there is always this downside to consider. It seems incumbent on us to evaluate all such trips even more carefully, ensuring that those undertaken have maximum possible benefits, outcomes and impact on students.

Teacher exchange or study visits are also becoming more established as ways to broaden perspectives and experience. These can also have considerable impact on global citizenship development within a school—directly on the teachers, and indirectly through their impact on colleagues and students.

A global citizen's checklist for school trips abroad

Why?

- What *unique* opportunities does this particular visit provide for development as a global citizen, in terms of the location, event or opportunity to see the impact of a global issue at first hand, or to meet people?
- What particular learning outcomes/enduring understandings/benefits do you hope will result from the visit—for students and, where applicable, staff?
- To what extent can these learning experiences be provided by other means (online conferences, visits to a less costly or closer location)?

- What are the benefits to the school community—students, staff, and the wider community?
- Visits are sometimes used to raise a school's profile and prestige. Is this a consideration in this visit?

To think about

- On what basis will participants be selected, or choose to take part?
- Are there any negative consequences of limited participation—to the people who do not take part; to the participants?
- How can other students, staff or the wider community benefit from the visit?
- Are the potential benefits commensurate with the costs in terms of time (including preparation) and money?
- What is the ecological impact of the visit? Are there ways this can be minimized? Should carbon offset be considered?

  Paying a small amount to finance projects that reduce carbon emissions elsewhere to offset the emissions produced by air travel is becoming more widespread. But does it work? Offsetting should be additional (that is, taking place because of our investment, not something that would have happened anyway) and lead to verifiable emissions reductions (Goodall 2007).

For service-related visits (see pages 136–138)

- How is the host community involved in planning?
- What benefits will the visit have to the host community?
- How can the visit be planned so that the visiting school and host communities are equally involved?

Getting the most out of a visit

- How can the visit be planned and structured to provide maximum positive impact on students?
- What preparation will maximize the effectiveness of the visit as a learning experience for global citizenship?
- How can participants be encouraged to engage with deeper level rather than surface culture?
- Can individuals be encouraged to develop a personal, individual set of outcomes they wish to achieve?
- How can you encourage students to reflect and learn actively during the visit, rather than simply participate physically (for

example, diary, learning log, daily emails to someone not on the visit; or daily brief discussions of what has been learned)?

- How will you be able to recognize and assess the extent to which learning outcomes/enduring understandings have developed?
- How can positive impact on the members of the school community who did not take part be maximized? How can any negative aspects or concerns be mitigated?

International Studies is a travel-based programme initiated by the Prince of Wales Collegiate, Newfoundland, Canada, which aims to provide meaningful cultural immersion for participating students. Full materials and suggestions for others wishing to implement a similar programme are available online at http://www.pwc.k12.nf.ca/cida/index.html archived at http://www.webcitation.org/5ZCkpeZOS.

▶ **How has travel impacted on your personal view of the world?**
▶ **What travel experience had the most impact on you?**
▶ **What implications does your experience of travel have on your involvement in educating students for global citizenship?**

CASE STUDY

OURIEL RESHEF/AMERICAN SCHOOL OF PARIS/ FRANCE

Model United Nations in a nutshell

Model United Nations, an authentic simulation of the UN General Assembly and its committees, catapults students into the world of diplomacy and negotiation. Students step into the shoes of UN ambassadors to debate issues on the organization's vast agenda. Students ("delegates") plot strategies, negotiate, debate and seek to resolve conflicts, while navigating the UN's complex "rules of procedure"—all in the interest of mobilizing international cooperation to resolve problems that affect almost every country on Earth.

Every year 100–150,0000 students participate in over 400 conferences, held in more than 50 countries, each involving between 200 and 3,000 students. Conferences are held in English, French or Spanish.

Each conference is the culmination of several months of hard work. Students research the needs, aspirations and foreign policy of the country they will "represent". Delegates are asked not to represent their own countries, with inestimable educational benefits. They formulate position papers, draft resolutions, and write speeches (in appropriate diplomatic language). Students research issues on the agenda and the position of various countries, learn rules of procedure, and develop progressive mastery of public speaking skills and elements of rhetoric.

At the conference, meeting with students from other countries and other cultures is immensely stimulating because the delegates have to be flexible and empathetic in order to develop the essential qualities for future citizens: a keen ear and an open mind —both needed to reach constructive common solutions.

The Model United Nations programme is *student-run*. Teachers are mere "advisors", and new students in the programme are instructed by their more experienced peers. Proactive students have opportunities to move up in the hierarchy of positions—from small to bigger and more challenging conferences, perhaps chairing committees of increasing size. At the apex are executive teams in charge of organizing conferences. As Secretary General, or one of the most senior assistants, students can bring a project of some magnitude to fruition. A true model of empowerment!

All involved agree that these conferences are a real character-building exercise for participants. All will retain a sense of being a world citizen and the conviction that, if goodwill alone is not enough to solve all the problems in the world, it is at least essential, and is nurtured in such conferences.

For further information visit http://www.cyberschoolbus.un.org/modelun/index.asp.

CASE STUDY

The Global Issues Network

The Global Issues Network (GIN), started in 2004 by six international schools in Europe, has rapidly grown to involve many more schools. Its mission is to help students realize they can make a difference by empowering them to work internationally with their peers to develop solutions for global issues.

In GIN, students engage in *real issues* needing *urgent attention*—it is not a simulation. Activities are collaborative not competitive. Students work with adults and professional networks and establish, use and maintain their own networks through communication technology. Importantly, students take ownership and leadership of the programme, coming to realize that adults don't have all the answers.

The principal activities of the GIN have been the organization of student conferences, and ongoing electronic communication ("town meetings"). At conferences (held in Europe each year since 2006 and in Beijing in April 2008) groups of students give presentations on projects they have been working on in their schools. They are joined by speakers, including youth activists and established figures, who contribute keynote and other sessions. Student presentations at recent conferences included "Waste Not, Want not?", "Fighting Against Child Prostitution" and "A South African School's Journey to Greening our Campus". Discussions are also held, with an emphasis on subsequent action. Carbon offsets mitigate the ecological downside of the travel to the conferences.

▶ **What roles can simulations play in educating for global citizenship?**
▶ **What are the benefits and drawbacks of simulations in this context?**
▶ **How can learning from simulations be transferred to other contexts or to real-life situations?**

School partnerships

In the last chapter we considered programmes that involve schools collaborating on online projects in the classroom. Establishing more extensive links between schools in different countries for more general purposes has also become much more widespread, encouraged by associations or authorities (for example, by NAIS in the USA, and by the UK government). Schools, often one in a developed country and one in a less developed country, may engage on projects together and student and teacher visits may be arranged. Various organizations assist in arranging partnerships, or schools establish their own links.

Good partnerships can generate enthusiasm and motivation for learning, action and positive change. They can engage whole school communities positively, providing transforming experiences for students and teachers in both schools. New perspectives and relationships can be developed. People view the world, and other people, in a different way. Overall, they can provide real benefit to both partner schools. Oxfam (2007) notes that, at their best, partnerships can help students develop many attributes directly related to global citizenship.

But cautionary voices are emerging. The very differences that potentially make such partnerships enriching and fulfilling present certain challenges that need to be fully considered. Margaret Burr, speaking with over 20 years' experience in school linking, comments: "There is a perception ... that linking is a 'good thing', and it is difficult for those who have not looked closely at links to understand that the reality may be very different to that which is envisaged." Unless very carefully considered and planned, links can fail and, at worst, actually result in negative experiences for all concerned. Oxfam (2007) notes the risks. Pity and sympathy rather than empathy and solidarity for people in the poorer partner school may develop in the more affluent partner. Stereotypes can be reinforced and paternalistic attitudes and feelings of superiority can develop. The sensitivities involved are highlighted by the following quotations from people from southern hemisphere schools involved in linking:

> *"When you come to us you are a visitor, when we come to you we are a resource."*
>
> *Ghanaian teacher, in Burr*

> *"First you came to us as missionaries, then you came to us as colonizers, now you come to us as linkers."*
>
> *Quoted in Burr*

> *"We thought we were OK until our partners described us as poor."*
> *Gambian linker quoted in UKOWLA (2006)*

On occasions well-established arrangements are abruptly ended when the school head changes, and the partner school is left upset. In links between "Northern" ("developed") and "Southern" ("less developed") countries, the effects on the southern partner if a link fails can be particularly damaging.

Burr notes that very little research on linking has been undertaken and there is little evidence of benefits to partners in either North or South. Nevertheless, principles of good practice in partnerships are emerging. These include:

- clear, shared motivation for the partnership between partners
- institutional commitment that goes beyond the enthusiasms of particular individuals
- mutual respect between the partners
- recognition that partners are equal, but different
- sustainability, in terms of staffing, funding, time
- clear benefits to both partners.

Oxfam (2007) describes four cornerstones for successful partnerships:

- commitment to an equal partnership with educational aims
- effective communications
- commitment to partnership learning through the curriculum
- good whole-school practice in education for global citizenship.

Charitable giving raises particular difficulties in partnerships and can work against notions of mutual respect and equality. Differences in material conditions can obscure the many other differences, such as quality of relationships, strength of community and levels of satisfaction and happiness. In some cases unwanted old clothes or obsolete computers have been offloaded on economically less advantaged partner schools. Even if money or useful items are provided, good practice indicates that this must be done within a context of interdependence rather than dependence. Some schools have now established trading links with their partner schools, selling jewellery or other items on behalf of the partner school. In some instances, the only financial transaction is for the more affluent school to raise funds to contribute towards the travel costs of students and staff from the partner school to visit them. Commenting to me on the need for considerable sensitivity in establishing links, the teacher in charge of linking her school in the UK with one in Africa noted: "We are linked to a richer school in the same city, as well as to a school abroad, so we know what it is like to be the poorer partner." Best practice now suggests that schools are well advised to consider linking with another school in their own country before attempting to form a partnership with a school overseas. This gives the opportunity to learn about the processes and principles of good partnering, before adding an additional level of complexity.

While the benefits of linking may be considerable, schools are well advised to think before and during the process of linking.

Rather different are the links developed between schools in different countries through such connections as the network of IB World Schools, the Global Connections Foundation (which organizes annual seminars for school leaders) and membership of Round Square (based on the theories of educationalist Kurt Hahn). All of these are implicitly or explicitly concerned with developing global citizenship in students.

Key questions

▶ Does your school have links with schools in your own country?

▶ If so, on what basis were these set up? If not, would your school benefit from linking with a different school in your own country, perhaps with a different social, cultural or ethnic composition?

▶ Does your school have links or partnerships with schools in other countries?

▶ If so, on what basis are they established?

▶ Are they based on mutual respect and equality?

▶ What attitudes do the partnerships encourage or develop in students

• in your school?

• in the partner school(s)?

▶ What are the feelings about the partnership(s) in your school? In your partner school(s)?

▶ How do you know?

Helpful and practical publications on school linking include Margaret Burr's *Thinking about Linking*, the Department for International Development's *Partners in Learning* (Oxfam 2007) and the UKOWLA *Toolkit for Linking* (2006). Although related to the UK context, they are of much more general relevance.

11 Global citizen action

Unless the global citizens we are educating are enabled and motivated to take action of some kind, all our efforts are futile. In our work with students we need to be able to counter feelings of doom and gloom at the global picture with hope and a sense of empowerment to make a difference. To do this, we need to assist students to develop the skills and knowledge to be able to do something useful and to encourage a desire to act for change. Their energy unleashed by informed concern and compassion needs to be channelled into appropriate action. We can help with this. As a result, we hope they will develop a view of themselves as people who *can* make a difference, and acquire an appetite for action—both well directed and effective.

But we must not rush into action. Harm can be—and has been—caused by entirely well meaning but hasty and ill-considered action. Even fund-raising has its downsides, if overused (Oxfam 2008). Sometimes, an appropriate response to a "Now what?" question can be "Undertake further research to become better informed". Action may come later.

We should certainly be encouraging students to take action as global citizens both inside and outside school. But our work needs to be reflective, sensitive, and carefully thought through.

Global citizen action can take various forms, in and out of school, and a simplified categorization is given in Table 11.1.

How we organize action indicates its importance within the school. Is it a central part of our activities, or confined to times after school and at weekends, with a few teachers only? Is it mandatory or voluntary? In some schools, notably the United World Colleges, community service plays a major part in ethos and activities, viewed more as an unquestioned part of the experience rather than as an imposition. Our intention must be to try to develop in students a likelihood of undertaking voluntary action when any requirements come to an end, and this should direct our thinking.

Action clearly has a global dimension when it involves encountering different cultural perspectives within our own communities or working on projects (such as with immigrants or refugees) that relate to global

Actions taken at a personal level	Actions that provide benefits to others directly or indirectly				Actions to benefit others indirectly, or encouraging action in others
	Indirect benefits to others			*Direct service or benefit to others*	
Personal lifestyle changes eg reduction in carbon emissions; ethical shopping	Community participation/ contributing to day-to-day operations of communities eg voting; membership of school or neighbourhood committees	Fund-raising eg arranging bake sales or fashion shows to raise funds for charities	Actions that do not involve a direct personal service, but indirectly benefit others eg voluntary administra-tive work for a charity organization: constructing a school for a community overseas	Providing a direct benefit or service to others eg teaching; cooking and serving meals for homeless people; visiting elderly people; writing to prisoners	Activism or political action eg lobbying for a particular cause; taking part in a demon-stration; membership of an action group; membership of an international lobbying organiza-tion such as Avaaz

Table 11.1

issues. Crucially, other forms of local action become action with a global dimension when reflected upon from a base of informed awareness of global issues. This is perhaps most obvious in environmental action—but applies to many other types of action too. The global is in the local once we have adopted what Harriet Marshall (2005) calls the "global gaze"—making the connections, and seeing how what we do relates to a bigger picture.

Some schools arrange action with a global dimension outside their own country. International service experiences can be truly transformative, as later case studies show. However, we must be wary of being seen to glamorize the global by associating it too heavily with trips to foreign parts. If they receive too much focus "the global" can come to be associated with the distant, the exotic and the occasional, not an integral part of everyday life. We become focused on the "there and then" not the "here and now", and their interconnections.

We cannot recognize global citizenship in the action itself. Consider clearing rubbish from a local recreation area. This benefits others, but it can be done under duress, as a punishment, or for money, with no interest in or understanding of the ecological importance of the work. It is distinguished as citizen action when it is done voluntarily or willingly, and with understanding of its importance to the community—that is, with citizenship intention. A global dimension is introduced when the action is viewed with a global gaze.

Similarly, action does not mean learning is involved. Students will not necessarily learn much from clearing rubbish, whatever the community benefits. Similarly, arranging a successful fund-raising disco does not necessarily indicate or raise awareness and understanding of the cause being supported. Indeed, a student could be involved for social reasons in raising funds for a charity concerned with poverty, without any challenge to views that poverty is self-induced or results from laziness.

Key questions

▶ How important is it for students to understand the context and importance of their action?

▶ How important is learning in global citizen action facilitated by schools?

▶ Is it acceptable for students to undertake work to benefit others when they themselves benefit or learn little from the experience?

▶ In global citizen action, what should the balance be between student learning and community benefits?

▶ To what extent should service activities be about developing habits of volunteering?

In the USA the focus on schools as learning institutions has given rise to the developing concept and tradition of "service learning", taken up as "active learning in the community" in the UK, and reflected in the IB approach to service in the Diploma Programme. The examples above become service learning relevant to global citizenship when students learn about the global background to the production and elimination of rubbish and its impact on the environment, or learn about and reflect on poverty, its causes and eradication, and how the disco money they raise is used for this.

Global citizen action is distinguished by the intention and the "global gaze". In schools, learning and personal development should be emphasized. The following list draws on Oxfam (2008), Potter (2002) and on practice in community participation in the USA, notably the National Service-Learning Clearinghouse, and the National Youth Leadership Council Learning Standards (2008).

Global citizen action in schools:

- is an authentic real-life experience
- stems from and develops knowledge and understanding of global issues
- relates to students' interests and motivations
- is set in a context relating to local–global communities of the participant
- is undertaken with appropriate, informed intentions
- provides students with rich and meaningful learning opportunities about the processes involved in taking action, and about themselves
- provides opportunities for students to develop appropriate attitudes and values
- exercises key skills such as critical thinking, project management and communication
- provides opportunities to learn and exercise new skills, take risks and undergo personal development
- engages students as active participants in as many ways as possible, including initiating and directing action
- is integral to the curriculum (academic or otherwise)
- is appropriate for students of all ages
- encourages or requires students to engage in reflection and self- or peer-assessment activities.

On this model, global citizen action is not an add-on or occasional deployment of useful youthful labour. It draws on and develops skills directly relevant, but not restricted to academic work. It provides particularly rich and potentially challenging opportunities for students to become engaged, because of the importance of the global issues, their complexity, and the real-life context.

Fund-raising

Fund-raising is a common activity in schools. Best practice now indicates it needs to be done thoughtfully, and in the context of learning. Students learn about the work of charities in relation to a broader and deeper understanding of the issues they are trying to address and how they do this. They come to understand how fund-raising fits into the broader picture of personal commitment and responsibility, and of (often political) change needed to resolve the issues. This counters simplistic and undesirable notions of dependence, "helping poor people" and solving global issues by application of cash. Oxfam (2008) has a helpful guide on this area.

Community service

Community service can have a uniquely powerful impact on students. It is a feature in many schools, and may be the focus of school-initiated global citizen action. To Malcolm McKenzie, "Genuine community service builds in the heart a feeling for and knowledge of human interdependence. Without this, no sense of community, no understanding of global connections, no real global citizenship are possible" (2004: 7). Bill Johnston (2008) comments: "Students are more comfortable with the concrete than the abstract, and working directly with those who need help/support has a tremendous impact on ability to understand when then confronted with films and discussions on such topics as genocide or global warming." International research (Yates and Younis in Davies 2006) indicates that for community service to have an impact it must lead participants to see themselves as people who can have an influence, and help them develop the knowledge and skills they need to do so.

Good practice highlights certain important features. The needs of the community should be identified by the community itself, and not imposed by the school or service providers based on their perceptions of need. Good projects are mutually beneficial to the community and the young people involved, who learn while providing a needed and valued service. Projects are often best undertaken by groups, with the possibility of teachers and students working alongside each other on an equal footing. Practice in the USA suggests the advantage of developing clearly defined projects that meet a need and come to an end. The successful completion is celebrated by both service providers and the community more generally.

Community service abroad can provide students with opportunities to develop new cultural perspectives, see the impact of global issues in other contexts, and benefit from meeting people with different outlooks and experience. But overseas service brings with it an additional level of complexity, as understanding of the community context is limited. Evidence is beginning to emerge of overseas projects undertaken by schools with the best of intentions but unfortunate consequences. Good practice is highlighting the fact that responding to the community's own perceived needs is particularly important. Undertaking a project without full community participation may reflect, and develop in students, patronizing attitudes. Schools are not development agencies, and students are not development professionals. Working closely with NGOs or other local organizations with strong experience on the ground is beneficial. The issue of sustainability is also important. Projects that require longer-term involvement should only be undertaken when the school makes the appropriate commitment.

> ▶ **What actions do you take as a global citizen?**
> ▶ **What have you learned from your own experience of community service or volunteering?**
> ▶ **What can you draw from your own experience that is relevant to community service in schools?**

Community service provides ample opportunities for "deep learning" experiences for students. They are also some of the most complex learning experiences for schools to organize or facilitate. Professional development is likely to be particularly valuable, therefore. While many schools require students to undertake service activities, many teachers may not be engaged with these personally, except when they are working with students. (See also Naye 2003.)

Developing student skills

Building Decision Skills is a short programme from the Institute for Global Ethics in the USA to teach ethics in middle and high schools (ages 12–18). Leming (2001) researched the programme in a context where it was implemented as part of service learning. The What Works Clearinghouse (a US Department of Education initiative) reviewed the research evidence and concluded that the programme had "potentially positive effects in the knowledge, attitudes and values domain" (2006). The programme can be slanted to give greater emphasis to global concerns and issues. Elementary Decision Skills is a corresponding programme for elementary schools. Activities lead students from ethical awareness to putting ethics into action.

The following case studies illustrate how global citizen action can be effectively managed in schools. First, Janet Yao reminds us of the importance of starting with the local, and of the opportunities for service to develop greater cultural awareness.

CASE STUDY

JANET YAO/BEIJING WORLD YOUTH ACADEMY/CHINA

Starting locally with global citizenship action

To start out being a global citizen one has to start out small—with the people around you. This is exemplified through the community service activity "English corner". It brings global citizenship down to a community scale. It is an exchange of culture, where students teach the English language to the people of the host community, but also share Western culture with them. Because the people being taught are adults, the students in return learn about Chinese culture, and develop a more global view.

One summer a group of students went to a small farming village in He Nan province, to do a small culture exchange project with the local school. They had access to all areas of the village and to some of the homes of the people in that village. They were able to experience first-hand the environment of individuals living in undeveloped areas.

Through the service programme, students are able to see and experience atmospheres and emotions that they would not encounter on a normal basis, which makes them more knowledgeable about the world around them. This, in turn, makes them willing to contribute to the betterment of humanity by taking action.

The following case study illustrates many aspects of best practice in service projects outside the school's own community, and the transformational potential of service learning.

CASE STUDY

BARRY DRAKE/CHINESE INTERNATIONAL SCHOOL/ HONG KONG, CHINA

Transformational learning through service

Each October, the formalized curriculum is put on hold for a week, and students in years 9 to 12 (ages 15–18) commit themselves to a range of "beyond the classroom" opportunities. These include taking part in service-learning projects in various Asian countries. All the projects seek to develop greater understanding of poverty and sustainable development, as well as fostering mutual cultural understanding. CIS staff and students are expected to develop sustainable long-term relationships with their service partners and to reflect on the learning gained from such experiences. Such projects aim to take students out of their comfort zones and, through experiential engagement, provide truly transformational experiences.

CIS's approach to service-learning projects is perhaps best epitomized in its work with the Miao village of Fang Xiang in Guizhou province, China. Here, in 2006, students completed their third engagement with the NGO Zigen, supporting education for minority-group girls in rural China.

Over the last two years, as requested by their NGO partners, CIS staff and students have helped provide specific training to teachers in the Fang Xiang village school. This has included the introduction and application of alternative teaching practices focusing on student-centred approaches to experiential learning activities. In 2006 Zigen suggested students help the village address "eco-tourism" possibilities. The team lived for the week in the remote village and, using global positioning equipment and laptop computers brought from Hong Kong, worked with students from Fang Xiang to produce an inventory of the village's eco-tourism assets. Three full-colour "tourist" booklets were produced in English and Putonghua, providing a clear map of the village for the first time and identifying areas of interest to prospective tourists.

Fang Xiang and CIS students worked collaboratively on this project, in which there was clear joint ownership, but time was also set aside for hands-on practical sessions aimed at exploring the students' respective cultures. Pre- and post-trip questionnaires were aimed at helping students identify attitudinal change. A survey showed overwhelmingly that the project helped to change students' level of intercultural understanding, as encapsulated in the comments below.

"Before this trip I believed that poverty depended on whether a person worked hard or not. But now I know that poverty depends a great deal on education."

"Before this trip I thought that there is poverty in the world because some people are lazy and because of this I didn't really support them. Now I know it's not the people's fault. They try their best but sometimes it isn't enough. Sometimes it's the climate's fault, sometimes the government's."

(Adapted from an article in *is* magazine (Volume 10, issue 1, Autumn 2007))

The next case study describes students undertaking leadership roles in peace initiatives.

CASE STUDY

ANTHONY SKILLICORN/UNITED WORLD COLLEGE OF SOUTH EAST ASIA/SINGAPORE

Initiative for Peace programme

Students can actively promote reconciliation and lessen prejudice in areas of conflict if given the right training. The Initiative for Peace programme at UWCSEA aims to promote permanent youth-led conflict management organizations, initiated by student-led conferences. It measures its success by what action participants at conferences undertake on their return home. As a direct result of the inaugural Kashmir Conference in June 2002 the organization Youth Initiative for Peace (IfP) was established in India and Pakistan. Sri Lanka Conferences in 2003, 2004 and 2005 established and consolidated Voice for Peace, a youth-led organization that contributed to the reconciliation process in Sri Lanka. The selection of Timor Leste as the 2007 focus was the first time IfP had chosen a post-conflict area, and this was repeated in 2008.

UWCSEA student members of Initiative for Peace spend a year being trained as facilitators and planning these week-long conferences. They send applications out, select participants, plan the conference programme and activities, and find and invite speakers. Participants are selected on the basis of their commitment to community service, leadership, and the perceived potential of their working to promote reconciliation and a reduction of prejudice in their area of conflict. IfP also strives to ensure a gender balance, and representation from as many local areas and organizations as possible. All accepted participants are awarded a bursary to cover all conference costs. Those accepting have to adhere to a number of criteria, which ensure that the conference is serious in tone and outcome.

UWCSEA students then facilitate and run the conferences, supported by six members of the teaching staff. The leadership shown by the student facilitators illustrates to the participants that young people are capable of playing an important role in community initiatives. The conference starts with trust building and presentation skills activities, then progresses to an academic study of specific issues and conflict resolution theory before finishing with focused planning of action-based community activities that the participants will undertake on their return. Building trust and friendships across conflict lines is often a first step in the search for ways to facilitate reconciliation and a commitment to action. The students are given opportunities to demonstrate leadership and to ensure that the mission statements of the college and the IB organization are put into practice.

Year 11 students who join the IfP activity meet at least once a week for an hour and a half throughout the school year to gain facilitation skills and undergo negotiation training. Twenty students are selected to be facilitators and run the conference in the first week of their holiday in June. Facilitators receive at least 12 hours of training from top negotiation experts and are taught facilitation skills by personal management coaches. The professional trainers give their services free of charge as they have such faith in the IfP model.

Although increasing numbers of schools are undertaking international service projects, direct participation is often limited. The following case study describes how follow-up after students returned from a project ensured that the whole school became involved.

CASE STUDY

MARTINA HEDGES/BROADGREEN INTERNATIONAL SCHOOL/LIVERPOOL, UK

The impact of an international project on the school as a whole

In February 2008, eight students from year 12 together with three staff worked in tribal and remote schools in Kerala, South India, in the school's first international service project. On their return, a DVD was produced in which the students recounted their expectations, experiences and even fears. This became a very powerful device to connect with the rest of the school: here were eight members of the school community doing extraordinary things thousands of miles away. Students arranged and delivered assemblies to all year groups, allowing all students and staff to share in their experiences—with considerable impact on peers and teachers.

The initial Indian project has cascaded into a number of developing international themes. The whole school is now involved in a humanitarian Red Cross project, and a number of students have expressed interest in a Tanzania project. The DVD was shown at a "Taste of India experience" organized in school by our local Indian community—and it may be shown on the city-centre plasma screen, widening the impact even further.

Among the students, a small group of "travellers" directly experience the country; a larger group are "actively involved" in international projects (and from this group the next travellers will probably emerge); and a final group are "partially involved" with a good awareness of the school's international aims and objectives. The aim is for the numbers of travellers and actively involved students to increase, as the school's international ambitions are realized.

The following case study describes work to develop and embed a school's service programme more effectively, and to give greater attention to meaningful assessment and reflection.

CASE STUDY

LAURIE KUCHIRKA/BRANKSOME HALL/TORONTO, CANADA

Strengthening a community service programme

In an effort to make the community service programme educational and cohesive, the school organizes each year around a theme. Last year, students were challenged to bring forth projects around "The fight against poverty". The community service council, made up of representatives from each year of the middle and senior schools, developed whole-school awareness and volunteer or fund-raising opportunities each month in line with the theme. For example, the school joined in World Vision's 30-hour famine, with the council organizing both the event itself and an awareness campaign. Next year, the school plans to focus on health and global infectious disease. By taking up a new theme each year, students are exposed to many important issues before they graduate.

There are plans to build in more reflective self- and informal teacher and supervisor assessment for independent volunteer opportunities across all year levels. In the past, supervisor assessment for students in years 9–10 has sometimes lacked constructive feedback, with such comments as, "She was a great help". Assessments in years 11 and 12 have been more effective as they are criteria-based. The aim is to build in more specific assessment criteria for years 9 and 10 also, using a rating scale for such skills as working collaboratively, persevering, and remaining committed to the organization. There is also a scheme to further encourage students to develop their own service action plans on issues of interest within the overall theme, rather than simply focusing on finding ways of completing their mandatory IB service hours.

From the personal to the political

Our notion of a global citizen recognizes that the everyday lives of people in many parts of the world have implications for the lives of others and for the environment. Responsible global citizens adjust their lifestyle accordingly. Action of this type forms the first column in Table 11.1, at the start of this chapter. As students get older, they are increasingly able to exercise such choices. As educators, we can raise awareness, encourage students to research the impact and implications of their personal lives on global issues, and to acquire the tools to consider whether they should take action. While "service" has an established place in school-organized activities in many schools, work that relates to the personal lifestyle choices of the global citizen is perhaps less common. In most schools, students' service action is likely to involve a relatively small proportion of their week. In contrast, lifestyle choices permeate all aspects of life, both in and out of school. Not addressing students' lifestyle choices appears to limit global citizen action unreasonably.

But focusing on what we can bring about as individuals, whether in lifestyle choices or through action more generally, is limiting in another way. There is a danger that we do not give sufficient attention to the bigger picture. Indeed, we can distort reality by becoming preoccupied with our own immediate concerns and impact, and develop an unrealistic view of their importance. Global issues are global because everyone is involved and affected, including big players on the global stage. Recognizing this is part of "understanding how the world works", as Oxfam (2006a) puts it. Focusing too much on personal lifestyle and action focuses on the tip of a large iceberg. Cutting down on food waste or recycling packaging in our personal lives does nothing to reduce the very considerable waste in the system producing and distributing our food. We must be concerned about the whole system of which our personal lives are a tiny part. There is no escaping the fact that global issues are political and often need political solutions. Committed global citizens are likely to want—perhaps should be encouraged—to become engaged in political activity to bring about the sort of changes they wish to see in the world. Hence, the last column in Table 11.1. Schools need to give careful consideration to the implications of this.

Key questions

▶ If community service is a school requirement, how can student motivation, responsibility and engagement be promoted?

▶ How important is it for students to undertake service for the right reasons?

▶ Does the curriculum in your school promote or facilitate taking global citizen action in connection with the academic curriculum?

▶ Are there ways in which the links between the academic curriculum and action could be enhanced?

▶ What factors make this more difficult? How might these be overcome?

▶ What forms of global citizen action does your school encourage?

▶ How do you develop the "global gaze" in locally based action?

▶ Should schools encourage all types of global citizen action equally, including personal lifestyle change and political activism?

▶ If so, what are the implications? If not, why not?

A thrust of this chapter is that meaningful action needs to embrace learning about global issues and about how to take effective action. Simultaneously, students learn more about themselves and others. If learning is to be encouraged in global citizen action, we need to be looking for evidence that it has taken place. This is becoming increasingly recognized, as, for example, in the recent IB (2008c) *Creativity, action, service guide*. This leads us into our next chapter, which considers further how we can assess global citizenship development.

12 Assessment and evaluation

The preceding chapters have focused on the actions we can take as educators to promote the development of global citizenship. But activity is not the same as effectiveness. How do we know what impact we are having on individual students? How do we know in what ways and how well they are developing as global citizens?

This leads us to consider assessment of the attributes of global citizenship. Juliette Mendelovits (2006) identifies four distinct reasons to assess global citizenship. Assessment is important because it:

- prompts us to sharpen up and communicate more clearly what we mean by the term "global citizenship", and what learning constructs and outcomes we are seeking to develop
- indicates that we value global citizenship
- allows us to monitor our effectiveness in developing global citizenship
- monitors students' progress to help us facilitate future learning.

Assessing the development of global citizenship is not going to be easy. We need to have a clear elaboration of what a global citizen is, or should be, to direct our activities—even though our understanding may be evolving. Banta et al (1996: 5) remind us that "institutional assessment efforts should not be concerned about valuing what can be measured but, instead, about measuring that which is valued." We need evidence on which to base any assessment. In assessing knowledge and some skills we are in familiar educator territory. But central to global citizenship are attitudes, values and predispositions to take action—quite a different prospect.

▶ How can we attempt to access attitudes and values?

▶ Even if we have a means to access them, how do we assess them?

▶ In assessing global citizenship, how important is it to assess actions?

▶ How do we assess actions that are done for the wrong reasons, or under a measure of compulsion or encouragement?

▶ Do we need to try to get beyond the actions to the underlying motivations for them, and also to the impact they have on the individual's values and attitudes?

▶ How can we do this?

Traditional assessment models confirm the role of teacher as expert, able to recognize and measure students in knowledge, skills and understanding. Our credibility as assessors is by virtue of our own education, training and expertise.

Key questions

▶ On what basis are we as educators in a position to assess global citizenship?

▶ Do we need to be credible, even good, global citizens ourselves if we are going to try to assess the development of global citizenship in our students?

▶ Is this the wrong model of assessment for global citizenship?

These are some of the reasons why this is difficult. But we must try.

Before looking at how the development of global citizenship might be assessed, it is helpful to remind ourselves about assessment in general.

- **Diagnostic assessment** determines the attributes that students already have and provides input for the teacher when planning future teaching.

- **Formative assessment** (often referred to as "assessment for learning" or "assessment for teaching") provides information to teachers and/or to students, to support and improve teaching and learning.

- **Summative assessment** ("assessment of learning" or "assessment of attainment") takes place at the end of a course of teaching in order to ascertain what has been learned by the students.

Key questions

▶ Does diagnostic assessment have a place in educating for global citizenship? If so, what form might it take? How might you carry it out?

▶ Do you consider that there is a place for summative assessment of global citizenship? If so, what would be its purpose? What would such an assessment be used for? What form might it take?

Summative assessment is sometimes used to select students and to distinguish between them in competitive situations. In educating for global citizenship, there is no need for losers. It is desirable for all of our students to emerge as better global citizens. So, there is a strong case for giving considerable attention to formative assessment. As global citizens their journey has only started. But the processes of formative assessment practised in schools can potentially assist in their continuing journey for the rest of their lives.

The central importance of formative assessment in effective learning is supported strongly by research evidence (Black and Wiliam 1998). An OECD report (2005) comments that: "The achievement gains associated with formative assessment have been described as 'among the largest ever reported for educational interventions'."

Approaches to assessment of global citizenship

Assessing global citizenship is a new field. The next chapter describes the only three initiatives I have encountered that specifically assess global citizenship. But, in devising our own instruments and methods, we can draw on good practice in formative assessment and learn from the experience of those countries that assess citizenship in general (OECD 2005; Eurydice 2005).

Research and good practice in related areas indicates that assessment of global citizenship should:

- engage students
- use a wide variety of situations and forms of assessment
- focus on contexts in which global citizenship is being shown
- focus on student activities that give indications of underlying students' attitudes and values
- where possible, relate to life outside school as well as in school contexts

- be constructive, positive and productive
- not be seen to be judgments of the worth or value of a student or their family
- support and be consistent with the school's overall approach to global citizenship.

Some approaches to use in assessing global citizenship development are outlined below.

Self- or peer-assessment

Self- or peer-assessment by students is an intrinsic and essential part of formative assessment, and has been used successfully with students from age 5 upwards. It should have a pivotal place in assessment of global citizenship development.

Self- or peer-assessment:

- places students at the heart of the assessment process
- develops skills that they can apply to all their activities, whether or not they are being formally assessed
- encourages them to become more objective about their work and action
- encourages continuing, regular reflection about their work and activities
- improves students' motivation to produce good work
- can be highly effective in raising standards, if used regularly
- is not a soft option
- requires careful and consistent training of students—for example, in how to make comments positive and constructive. Jerome et al (2003) offer suggestions on this.

It's worth noting that students are "generally honest and reliable in assessing both themselves and one another; they can even be too hard on themselves" (Black and Wiliam 1998). Research shows that students take seriously comments from their peers.

In some contexts peer-assessment can enable the teacher to focus on giving feedback to specific students rather than attempting to do so to all. It also has intrinsic merits. Black and Wiliam note that peer-assessment promotes self-assessment. Students acquire skills and an awareness of learning outcomes that they can apply to themselves.

Self- and peer-assessment can be used in written work done at class or at home, in oral work, and after discussions or collaborative activities. Assessment can be oral, in writing, open-ended or using a questionnaire. Peer-assessment can also be made by a group of students who have all reviewed a piece of work, or shared in the same activity.

Here are some examples of peer-assessment.

- After reading an article or short story or watching a film relating to poverty or slavery, students reflect on what they have learned about social injustice. They write their own reflection, or share it orally with a teacher, the class or with a peer.

- After a discussion, students reflect on what they learned about the process of reaching conclusions by discussion. They review the role they and others played in the discussion.

- After a collaborative project, students reflect individually on what they learned about working together, and then discuss this with peers. They can produce guidelines to improve collaborative work on the basis of their experience, or criteria for effective collaboration. These can then be used in future assessments.

Create a manifesto for global citizenship

Creating a manifesto, appropriate to the age of students, can assist in development and assessment by focusing everyone's attention on what is important. This is best developed collaboratively with students (possibly parents too). Post it in the classroom, or distribute it to students and parents as a leaflet. It could include:

- an agreed statement of what a global citizen is
- an elaboration of this to give characteristics shown by a global citizen, for example:
  - A global citizen is aware of/knows about ...
  - A global citizen cares about ...
  - A global citizen acts to ...
- examples of how global citizenship is addressed in school
- examples of how students can act as global citizens outside school
- quotes on global citizenship.

There could be core sections relevant to all students, and age-specific sections. This approach has been adapted from an idea by Tony Breslin of the Citizenship Foundation: visit http://www.citizenshipfoundation. org.uk.

Global citizenship portfolio

This might include the following.

- **Global citizenship file**—paper or electronic, in which work produced in connection with global citizenship is stored. It could also include newspaper cuttings, photographs, and the global citizenship manifesto.
- **Global citizenship journal**—journal or learning log (paper or electronic), in which students record activities, reflections and learning as a global citizen. This could include activities undertaken at school or out of school. This could be made distinctive by buying fair trade books for students to use.

Encourage reflection on global citizenship learning

Reflection is particularly appropriate in an area concerned with attitudes and values and can take many different forms. In oral work, reflection can be encouraged by requiring students to be silent for a short period before speaking. They can be asked to prepare their contributions by writing notes before they speak. Research indicates that the quality of contributions is increased.

Consider using the "three whats" sequence:

What? Description of what happened/what I did

So what? What I learned from this and why?

Now what? What are the implications of this? What will I do differently in the future? What action will I take? What are my future goals?

Reflective paragraphs or essays can be used in regular class and homework. For example, at the end of a topic that relates to global citizenship, students could answer questions such as: How do I feel about ...? What have I learned about myself from my study and experience of a different culture? For further ideas see Reed and Koliba (1995) on which this approach is based.

In global citizen action, encourage reflection with the following guiding questions.

What have you learned during this action about:

- global issues?
- the way other people see the world?
- how people interact?
- yourself?
- you and your communities?

Develop assessment rubrics for global citizenship

Rubrics are specific guidelines with criteria to assess the quality of student work or behaviour, usually on a scale. Rubrics can be used by teachers, students and in peer-assessment. Tables 12.1 and 12.2 are some examples of rubrics used in citizenship.

	Success criteria		
	Towards expectations	At expectations	Beyond expectations
How effectively can you participate in a group discussion?	Listen to others and speak at an appropriate time	Listen to others, speak at an appropriate time and respond to the opinions of others	Listen to others, speak at an appropriate time and respond to the opinions of others Stick to or amend an opinion in the light of others' arguments
How effectively can you consider a range of opinions?	Acknowledgment of others' viewpoints but little analysis	Understand and respond to others' viewpoints	Appreciate others' viewpoints and reflect on these when justifying own view

Table 12.1 For secondary students, aged 11–14 (Extracted from QCA (2006))

Integrity is represented by an upright character—honest, respectful, responsible, tolerant, sincere			
	Rarely	Sometimes	Most of the time
Is not easily swayed by peer pressure			
Does what is right, not what is popular, even in a difficult situation			

Table 12.2 For primary school children (note that integrity is defined within the rubic) (From Viroqua Elementary and Liberty Pole Center Parent-Student Handbook (2001))

Both rubrics emphasize positive achievement. They are not couched in negative terms —"student does not participate", "student is dishonest". The Viroqua example differentiates by the frequency with which positive behaviour is shown. In contrast, the QCA rubric distinguishes levels by qualitative differences in what students do.

Be collaborative, creative and experimental in assessment

In assessment of citizenship, global or otherwise, considerable flexibility and creativity is possible. It is also an area where it is appropriate to collaborate and coordinate between teachers and across subject departments.

- Brainstorm assessment ideas with colleagues.
- Involve students in devising forms of assessment and the actual assessment instruments. In some contexts, give students a free hand to demonstrate or record learning however they wish.
- Use a wide variety of evidence for assessment.

Evidence for assessment can include all of the following. For further ideas, see Jerome (2003), Jerome et al (2003) and Ord—from which some ideas are drawn.

Checklists	Questionnaires
Teacher observation	Teacher conversation with student
Parent input	Notes
Artwork	Blogs
Presentations	Tests
Participation in school events and activities	Input of other people who work with students
Peer-assessment of various types	General conduct in school
Performance in service activities	Working with others in various capacities
Performance in posts of responsibility (for example, student council) Making a video of a discussion or group work—students conduct self- and peer-assessment after watching it	Writing letters to represent views to school head, newspaper, politicians or public figures Add an extra short question related to global citizenship to tests and homework questions—assess responses using global citizenship criteria

Citizenship qualifications

Assessment of citizenship is mandatory in schools in England for students aged 11–14. Various qualifications are available to assess aspects of citizenship (including limited aspects of global citizenship) and promote their development throughout the secondary school. The criteria for assessment and assessment materials used in these qualifications may inform thinking about assessment of global citizenship at secondary level. Details of qualifications are available on the Quality Improvement Agency website: visit http://www.post16citizenship.org/assessment.

Qualifications include citizenship studies at GCSE and GCE AS and A2 levels (for students aged 16–18). Assessment is through controlled assessment (of supervised projects on an extended basis) and written examinations in varying proportions. Written assessment involves writing about active citizenship experience. AQA, the UK awarding body for general qualifications, offers both GCSE and GCE AS and A2: visit http://www.aqa.org.uk.

An example of a controlled GCSE assessment is available at http://www.qca.org.uk/qca_15723.aspx archived at http://www.qca.org.uk/qca_15723.aspx.

Key questions

▶ Who is the better global citizen

- a student who writes a carefully crafted and reasoned argument as to why we have no responsibility towards others whose basic needs are not met; or

- a student who is clearly moved by the plight of those less fortunate, and is committed to action, but expresses this less cogently and with many inaccuracies and errors?

▶ We are used to assessing the quality of expression and reasoning in oral and written work. But in assessing global citizenship, should we also pay attention to the views that are being expressed?

▶ If students and educators are all global co-citizens, is it appropriate for educators also to be assessed?

▶ Should assessment of global citizenship be a collective activity, in which students and teachers are all involved in making assessments and being assessed? Is "assessment" the most appropriate term to use here?

13 Programmes and awards

Schools should celebrate and give recognition to what they value, and this should certainly apply to global citizenship no less than other areas. Offering a recognition programme indicates the school's commitment. Conversely, not doing so may send other messages. Here we shall be looking at established programmes that seek to promote and offer some form of award or acknowledgment of the development or expression of global citizenship in individual students in schools. This is a very small field currently, so we shall begin by considering some programmes in related areas that may be helpful to schools who are considering developing a programme.

IB programmes aim to develop "international-mindedness" in students, and some initial research has been undertaken on their effectiveness in doing so (for example, Hinrichs 2003; Simandiraki and Yao 2004). But international-mindedness is not specifically assessed or evaluated in the Diploma Programme, for example. It can also be argued that global citizenship should go beyond international-mindedness as articulated by the IB.

The European Council of International Schools offers each member school the possibility of making an award for international understanding to one of its students each year. Similarly, the Council of International Schools International Student Award can be awarded to individuals or groups of students in each of its member schools for a project that contributes to "internationalism" in the school community. These awards are not for global citizenship as such, but for closely related characteristics. The East Asia Regional Council of International Schools offers a specific global citizenship award. But, however worthy the recipients, the programmes involve recognition of one or a few students only, and are therefore competitive to an extent. They are also awarded in retrospect, and in that sense do not directly promote development of students, but recognize characteristics already expressed.

ASDAN (Award Scheme and Accreditation Network) in the UK has pioneered a comprehensive array of awards in non-academic areas of student life. Although there is no award in global citizenship, a number are of general relevance, including International, Active Citizenship, Citizenship in Action, and Community Volunteering awards. Awards are related to the UK context but a number of non-UK schools are registered centres. The materials and approach may be of interest to schools developing their own programmes.

Boy Scouts of America offers a *Citizenship in the World* badge (US Scouting Service Project 2006). There is an emphasis on constitutional matters and academic research, which does not relate closely to global citizenship as we have described it.

Let us now look at programmes specifically designed to foster global citizenship as described here.

The Finnish Global Citizenship Maturity test

Launched in 1994, this initiative of the Finnish United Nations Association (UNA) is the earliest attempt I have encountered to promote and recognize the development of global citizenship. Open to anyone in the world, over 1,700 people aged 8 to 80 have passed it. The programme, lasting up to 10 weeks, involves self-directed learning individually or in groups. Participants select a theme for their work, and notify the Finnish UNA. They undertake research, approaching it from international, national, local and personal perspectives. Research is recorded in an in-depth study, and an accompanying diary is used for personal critical reflection. Having acquired a measure of expertise on the chosen theme, the participant (or group) communicates to others using any means, for example, directing a play, arranging meetings, writing articles, or organizing an exhibition. After self-evaluation, a comprehensive portfolio of materials is collated and sent off to the Finnish UNA, and satisfactory completion leads to the award of the certificate to the individual or group (Allahwerdi and Rikkinen 2002; Global Citizenship Maturity Test). At the time of writing it was unclear whether the programme is still active.

Qualifications in global citizenship

Cambridge International Examinations offers academic qualifications in global issues (as outlined in chapter 8), but currently, I know of no qualifications in global citizenship at school level. Higher education appears to be leading the way in this area with a number of institutions offering programmes, notably in North America. These include Lehigh, Franklin Pierce and Drake Universities, and the University of Delaware. These programmes are touched on here because they may give us ideas to use in our school contexts. They lead to certificates and may include required core courses, electives chosen from a range of courses with global elements, seminar participation, study abroad and service learning. Lehigh requires participation in an intersession travel experience during which students "experience the challenge of negotiating otherness" and are confronted with the "human face of globalization".

In Canada, the University of British Columbia, which gives considerable emphasis to global citizenship, offers an interactive online course on global citizenship to its students and to those of partner universities abroad.

The Academic Certificate of Global Citizenship at Mesa Community College, Arizona, comprises relevant academic courses plus research, study abroad or participation in the Model United Nations. Drake University's Global Ambassador Program, one of the most comprehensive, includes a course in intercultural communication, second language study, participation in events and activities related to global citizenship on campus or in the community, and service learning. It also includes a group learning experience in preparation for a group project to educate the campus and/or community about a global issue or cultural perspective.

Some universities are showing considerable commitment to promoting and recognizing global citizenship. Although, as indicated, there is a considerable and understandable academic core to the courses, some are innovative and give laudable attention to changes in perspective and practical action.

The following case study describes a programme in a school in Canada to recognize its students' involvement in "global education".

CASE STUDY

THE FATHER BRESSANI CATHOLIC SECONDARY SCHOOL/ONTARIO, CANADA

Global Education Certificate programme

The school was designated a School for Global Education by its board of education in 1997 and undertook a wide range of initiatives to enhance its global dimensions. Among these, regular courses were reviewed to incorporate global education elements and some were designated as "globalized". A "global co-op" programme was also introduced, in which students had four-month placements in a company, organization or NGO considered "global".

A programme was introduced offering a Global Education Certificate and plaque for graduating students who:

▶ enrolled in "globalized" courses
▶ fulfilled the school's community service requirement with a global dimension, or took part in the global co-op programme
▶ wrote a 2,500-word extended essay on a global topic.

A programme of the kind outlined above (based on a longer case study by De Caria et al (2004)) could be readily adapted to other school contexts. Here there is a substantial academic emphasis and the commitment to action related to global citizenship is limited. But it indicates how a programme of recognition of global engagement can be devised.

We now come to the only programmes I know of that are specifically concerned with promoting and recognizing the development of global citizenship in numbers of individual students in schools. (The EARCOS award is for a single student per school.) (I will be delighted to hear about any others.) The first, described in the case study below, is a well-established programme started by a school in Australia.

CASE STUDY

RAY BYWATERS/BANKSIA PARK INTERNATIONAL HIGH SCHOOL/SOUTH AUSTRALIA

Global Citizens Medal

From its inception in 2003, Banksia Park International High School has celebrated over 100 successful recipients of the school's Global Citizens Medal (GCM). The medal aims to develop students equipped with the capacities to operate as well-rounded citizens in an increasingly global world.

In establishing the medal, the school did not want yet another school prize or exclusive programme. The aim was to build social capital by celebrating students' investment and commitment to a range of activities in the local and global community. Therefore every student would have an opportunity to apply for a GCM.

Students are central to the process and are responsible for demonstrating that they meet the qualities outlined in the GCM Recipients Declaration. The first part involves the student using an electronic template to document/verify participation in local, state, national and global activities. Each student develops a GCM portfolio, and embedded personal reflection/self-assessment empowers students to recognize their qualities. Finally, students undertake a 15-minute presentation demonstrating their worthiness for the medal before a panel, which comprises a community member, a family member, teacher advocate, a "critical friend" from the senior year level and a junior school observer.

Critical to the programme's success is a dedicated manager/coordinator and a team of teachers, who mentor students in their GCM application and demonstration. Teachers involved remark that the process "adds to the confidence of the applicant", "provides extra encouragement and support", "enables students to recognize that we are proud of their non-academic achievements and appreciate their accomplishments" and "recognizes the caring that occurs between teachers and students".

An understanding of what the medal entails is promoted by involving members of the school's community in the final presentation/demonstration. A community member stated: "It gave me the opportunity to see first-hand the process and, in doing so, set me up as an advocate for the GCM." Another commented: "It gave community members, who may not be familiar with schools, the opportunity to see the high calibre of young people." Similarly family members, when asked to express the panel experience in one word, responded with "proud", "impressive", "privileged" and "enlightening".

By establishing a collaborative approach, underpinned by trust and caring, the final part no longer involves traditional tools of measurement and testing and instead is a genuine celebration of a student's citizenship. As one student reflected: "When it came to the demonstration I wasn't as worried or nervous as I thought. It helped knowing that I wasn't going to be graded."

Research indicates that Banksia Park International High School's Global Citizens Medal is successful because:

- ▶ all students can apply
- ▶ there is no limit on the number of GCM recipients
- ▶ the processes used are non-competitive
- ▶ students are responsible for, and involved in, the process
- ▶ one person is responsible for managing the whole process
- ▶ a team of teachers provide continuous support and guidance
- ▶ self- and group assessment affirms the application process
- ▶ school and community members are integral participants in the presentation/demonstration
- ▶ the demonstration process promotes the medal in the school and wider community
- ▶ a GCM high quality package (a presentation folder, engraved medal and personally signed parchment by the Federal Minister for

Education, Science and Training) has been developed collaboratively by students

▶ students are able to demonstrate their personal skills, understandings and dispositions in a real-life learning context.

The GCM is highly sustainable within the school. Another secondary high school in South Australia adopted the programme in 2005 and continues to attract student participation. Now in its sixth year, the GCM is a recognizable and intrinsic feature of Banksia Park International High School. For more information visit: http://www.bphs.sa.edu.au/wbpgs/1-10@24/10/docs/GlobalCitizen-final.pdf archived at http://www.webcitation.org/5XcNz1GsJ.

The second programme, while sharing much of the underlying thinking with the GCM, has a different approach.

The International Global Citizen's Award (IGC Award)

The IGC Award encourages and recognizes a commitment by individuals to develop as global citizens. It starts with and relates directly to the everyday lives of young people as global citizens now, and embraces both personal lifestyle and community engagement. The programme develops awareness, community participation skills and global citizen action, all in the context of continuing reflection, over a minimum of six months. It is concerned with nurturing new perceptions and perspectives, with attitudes and values, and different ways of seeing the world and others. The programme is open to participants aged 11 and over (with no upper age limit) and, although some of the activities may be undertaken in groups, the award is to individuals.

The IGC Award is an international grass-roots project, operated by individual centres (not necessarily schools), using a common model that they are helping to shape. Launched in Shanghai in November 2006, and piloted in the 2007–8 school year, it is being offered in 16 centres in 12 countries in 2008–9 (Roberts 2006, 2007, 2008).

The award promotes and recognizes change and development of individual students as global citizens, not the "standard" reached. It encourages and recognizes the quality of the journey—not distinction, academic attainment or outstanding leadership. The programme involves real, authentic engagement by students *in* global citizenship. It is voluntary (as it requires making lifestyle changes) and non-competitive. The more students who participate, develop and receive the award, the better.

Participants are fully involved in each centre's programme. Adults are mentors and guides, rather than "experts", and some schools are using non-teachers in mentoring roles. In Amman Baccalaureate School older students mentor younger students, and this is to become a key feature of the programme.

There are four areas of the programme.

1. Understanding other cultures and outlooks

While this can include reading, internet research, watching films or television, direct personal interaction is also required. Personal encounters can include talking to people in the school or local community (a structured interview format has been developed), or during international visits, or interactions with other IGC Award participants. It is the depth and quality of encounter that is important. Coming to appreciate something of the world view of others, our own is changed.

2. Personal global footprint

Participants research and review their impact—or "footprint"—in two areas of their daily lives:

- **being good with money**—the impact of how we spend our money on other people and the environment, and
- **environmental responsibility**—focusing on personal environmental impact.

After their research, participants consider and take action, for example, reducing their use of resources, recycling and changing buying habits.

3. Influence and involvement with others

This section is concerned with three ways in which students can work with others, in areas relevant to global citizenship:

- personal community service, including environmental action
- advocacy, persuasion or promotion—relating to an appropriate cause, for example, at home, among friends, within school, by writing to a politician
- active participation in decision-making processes, for example, in a group project, or the IGC Award itself.

4. Recording and reflecting on change

This pivotal element involves keeping a personal log or journal (in any format), in which participants reflect on developing knowledge, awareness and actions as a global citizen. Where appropriate, and within students' capabilities, this is intended to be hard-headed and to employ critical faculties fully. Participants are also encouraged to reflect on their experience of working with others and on their developing understanding of other cultures and perspectives, and themselves. This element is critical in encouraging and attempting to access development in attitudes and values.

Although ambitious in many ways, the award programme involves a limited time commitment, averaging around two hours a week. Depth of engagement and the impact of activities are therefore important. Relevant existing programmes and activities can be incorporated, including curriculum work, service elements and activities within organizations, for example, Roots and Shoots. However, it involves all participants in doing something new.

The initial programme, "bronze level", involves participation for a minimum of six months. Bronze recipients can proceed to more demanding "silver" and "gold" levels, developed by the project director and centres to form an overall progression. These involve increasingly challenging personal projects leading to action, and engagement in greater depth and focus with issues and other cultures. Participants in silver and gold will also act as mentors to bronze participants.

Any school with access to the internet can become a centre, and costs are low. Interactions between centres and with the central administration (currently voluntary) are electronic, and no travel is required. Each centre runs its own programme and makes its own awards using the common international model, but reflecting the local context. Centres are expected to share practice and ideas with others, to contribute to the development of the programme itself and to an evolving international understanding of global citizenship.

Centres include national, international, state, independent, IB and non-IB schools, and an organization concerned with service learning. Experience during the first year has been very encouraging, with over 150 participants receiving the award. Centres welcome the combination of flexibility and structure, but, following feedback, additional materials are being developed to assist in planning and student reflection for those centres wishing to use them. New ways for centres to share perspectives will also be trialled.

Participants have organized the first fair trade event in Qatar, convinced parents to change to energy-efficient light bulbs, helped to construct a school in Tanzania, given assembly presentations about global issues, and found out about Indian culture in the local community and in a visit to India. They have reflected, commenting that the award has stimulated them to do new things and to acquire new perspectives and understandings as global citizens. Perhaps surprisingly, one of the most common challenges has been developing students' understanding of other cultures, illustrating that simple membership of a diverse community does not necessarily lead to deeper intercultural understanding.

It is hoped that all participants who stay the course will receive the award. Participants share in the decisions on who receives the award, with mentors, and, in some cases, parents and others. Experience is that students are serious, fair and scrupulous. Some bronze level participants are engaged on the silver award from 2008, and gold will be introduced in 2009.

On the basis of the first year, centre coordinators comment:

> *"The project was an interesting one and ... the students were more internationally aware citizens than before they embarked on the project. It has encouraged them to participate in more international activities city-wide. The project has enriched and motivated the students on their personal global citizenship journey."*
> *Martina Hedges, Broadgreen High School, Liverpool, UK*

> *"The award has added to participants' experience and changed their view of their surroundings, making them aware of the need for a change and how they can make a difference."*
> *Abdel Razzaq Najjar, Amman Baccalaureate School, Jordan*

> *"When we found a subject/cause/topic that really fired our students, we were able to explore it in-depth and perhaps allow them to become passionate and involved in something they found worthwhile."*
> *Katrin Bizier, The English Academy, Kuwait*

> *"It's a wonderful opportunity for students to broaden their horizons and to gain exposure in those areas that are already so important to many of them. It's a wonderful complement to the academic experience that I imagine most of the participants are already undertaking."*
> *Leslie Lichtenstein, St Timothy's School, Stevenson, Maryland, USA*

Further details, including information on how to become a centre, are available at http://www.globalcitizensaward.org.

Conclusion: Grappling with the global

I hope this book has raised some questions, posed challenges and provided suggestions for how schools can more effectively educate for global citizenship. But it will only have done its job if it prompts some change on the ground and begins a continuing process. As we become increasingly aware of our interconnectedness and interdependence, as the human population inexorably climbs higher, as competition increases for limited resources, or as they become extinguished, as the gap widens between richer and poorer or healthy and unhealthy, as quite reasonable expectations and capacities to utilize more resources rise in certain countries, as biodiversity declines and as the planet shows signs of sustained abuse and overexploitation, the challenges increase.

Those of us in schools face a real challenge to our own activities and, indeed, our purpose. Offering a rigorous education to ensure transmission of knowledge and acquisition of skills for life and work in our new global world is important. But is our curriculum preparing students to consider and prepare for the responsibilities and challenges they will face increasingly in their lives—arguably on a scale not faced by previous generations? In some cases, doesn't the education we offer look suspiciously like what we were offered—for a different world 10, 20, 40 years ago? We occupy years of students' lives in our schools. Are we doing our best to work alongside them, to advise and accompany them to face the future—to face the situations we have created and they will have to resolve?

Whatever the increased challenges, we as educators have no more time to work with students. We have to make some serious choices about how we direct our efforts and allocate our time.

And through all of this, we need to maintain hope. We need, personally, to recognize the seriousness of the challenges we face, but also to be aware of positive changes and causes for optimism.

To conclude, here are a few practical suggestions for ways forward.

1. Start small with quick hits with obvious impact

This is the advice given in change initiatives in general. It certainly applies here. So, consider where you can have impact, with the minimum of effort on the shortest timescale. For example:

- arrange relevant displays
- make some changes in student classroom activities
- investigate fair trade sourcing
- increase recycling
- buy teaching and reference resources
- set up a budget for global citizenship education
- arrange some relevant assemblies
- arrange relevant professional development.

2. Work with others and enlist support within your school

Although you can go it alone, you will be far more effective if you are working with mutually supportive colleagues. Be canny in how you spend your time, and who with. Engage with some unexpected people as well as with those who might be expected to join in with initiatives such as this. And, of course, consider who has the power and influence, and try to get some of them involved.

3. Undertake a comprehensive, thorough, systematic audit in all areas

This is advice for a school as a whole, but it can also be applied to the immediate activities and sphere of influence of the individual. It is a good tactic to take stock before expending too much effort.

4. On the basis of the audit, develop a comprehensive implementation plan; work systematically through all levels and areas within the school

Again, what applies at the level of the school can also apply to the individual teacher trying to effect change within their own professional activities. Consider your classroom, your teaching style, the resources you use, as well as lesson content.

5. Look for obstacles and constraints

Are these reasonable? If not, work to remove them—wherever they are.

6. Exemplify consultative, open decision-making in all processes

Involve all staff and engage students and parents. Develop agreed means for reaching decisions and for resolving internal conflicts.

7. Include "educating for global citizenship" planning in the normal school development planning process

Monitor progress. Review successes and failures.

8. Remember that it is "mind shift" that will effect change

Provide training and support for yourself and others wherever and whenever necessary. Give prominence to professional development in all plans. Although money will be required for some things, the mind shift that is necessary if we are to be successful in educating for global citizenship is of overriding importance. Money should be expended to maximize mind shift.

9. Hang in there ... and connect with others

The species is waking up ... you are not alone. Things are moving. Connect with others on the move too—wherever they are.

As a species we are incredibly inventive, and have great capacity to effect change. We have demonstrated this conclusively in getting ourselves to our current situation. We are demonstrating it again as we grapple with the challenging issues our activities and actions have produced. We are beginning to see significant shifts in opinion—quite quickly—on matters such as climate change. And with electronic communication, we have a means to communicate and mobilize. One senses in some countries a longing for politicians to do more, and a grassroots frustration at limited commitment to address major issues. The Make Poverty History campaign was one such recent manifestation. One senses it may not be long before people take to the street over climate change.

So things are changing ... and fast. In trying to make a difference, network and connect with others who are interested. Share ideas, enlist and provide support.

So where does this leave us on Monday morning, returning to our desks and classrooms? As teachers, we can operate, often with considerable freedom, within our own classrooms. Writing our ideas down in an action plan is a way of thinking things through, and sometimes we feel more committed to things we have written down.

But recognize too, that working on your own in your own school or classroom is necessarily of limited scope. Consider your department, your school, the wider context, and how you can influence and work with others to do something—or something more— about educating for global citizenship. And if you feel constrained by an external curriculum, then let this be known. Curriculum bodies move slowly—and sometimes need a bit of urging along.

So from the centre of your web of connections, move, shake and make waves, and get your school to do so too.

Remember the wise words of the ancient Chinese sage Lao Tzu, founder of Taoism, and as relevant now as when they were written about 2,500 years ago:

> *"Even the longest journey must begin where you stand."*

Take heart from the words of Margaret Mead (1901–78), the US anthropologist and author:

> *"Never doubt that a small group of thoughtful, committed citizens can change the world; indeed, it's the only thing that ever has."*

And the last word must go to the inspiration and challenge of Nelson Mandela:

> *"Education is the most powerful weapon you can use to change the world."*

References and key further reading

Where there are references in the text to key documents on the internet, these have been archived. These can therefore be accessed even if they are not available on the original website.

Key further readings are indicated in bold. While written for national contexts, they are of more general interest and relevance.

Ackermann, L., Feeny, T., Hart, J., and Newman, J. 2003. *Understanding and Evaluating Children's Participation: A review of contemporary literature*. Plan UK/Plan International. Online at http://www.plan-uk.org/pdfs/literaturereview.pdf.

ACT! Active Citizens Today. http://www.tvdsb.on.ca/act/. Accessed 14 August 2008.

Alexander, R. 2008. *Towards Dialogic Teaching: Rethinking classroom talk* (4th edition). Thirsk, UK. Dialogos UK Ltd. See also http://www.robinalexander.org.uk.

Allahwerdi, H. and Rikkinen, H. 2002. "The Challenge to Global Citizenship: Study Program". In Zajda, J. I. (ed). *Society and the Environment: Teaching SOSE*. South Melbourne, Australia. James Nicolas Publishers.

Allen, K. 2004. *Developing Hearts & Minds in Relation to Global Dimensions*. Presentation to the Alliance for International Education conference. Düsseldorf, Germany. October 2004.

Allport, G. W. 1954. *The nature of prejudice*. Cambridge, Massachusetts. Addison-Wesley.

Appiah, K. A. 2006. *Cosmopolitanism: Ethics in a World of Strangers*. New York, New York: W. W. Norton. London, UK: Allen Lane.

Australian Sustainable Schools Initiative (AuSSI). http://www.environment.gov.au/education/aussi. Accessed 9 November 2007.

Award Scheme and Accreditation Network (ASDAN). http://www.asdan.org.uk/.

Banta, T. W., Lund, J. P., Black, K. E., and Oblander, F. W. 1996. *Assessment in Practice: Putting principles to work on college campuses*. San Francisco, California. Jossey-Bass.

Bell, A. C. and Dyment, J. E. *Grounds for Action: Promoting physical activity through school ground greening in Canada*. Toronto, Canada. Evergreen. Online at http://www.evergreen.ca/en/lg/pdf/PHACreport.pdf. Accessed 26 February 2008.

Best, D. L. 2004. "Robber's Cave Revisited: Lessons for Cross-Cultural Psychology". In Setiadi, B. N., Supratiknya, A., Lonner, W. J. and Poortinga, Y. H. (eds). *Ongoing themes in psychology and culture* (online edition). Melbourne, Florida. International Association for Cross-Cultural Psychology. Online at http://ebooks.iaccp.org/ongoing_themes/chapters/best/best.php. Archived at http://www.webcitation.org/5a2qeGXJH. Accessed 28 February 2008.

Black, P. and Wiliam, D. 1998. "Inside the Black Box: Raising Standards Through Classroom Assessment". *Phi Delta Kappan*. Vol 80, number 2. Online at http://www.pdkintl.org/kappan/kbla9810.htm. Archived at http://www.webcitation.org/5Ye8ATNYs.

Boix Mansilla, V. and Gardner, H. 2007. "From teaching globalization to nurturing global consciousness". In Suárez-Orozco, M. M. (ed). *Learning in the global era*. Berkeley and Los Angeles, California and London, UK. University of California Press.

Burnouf, L. 2004. "Global Awareness and Perspectives in Global Education". *Canadian Social Studies*. Vol 38, number 3. Online at http://www.quasar.ualberta.ca/css/ Css_38_3/ARburnouf_global_awareness_perspectives.htm. Archived at http://www. webcitation.org/5ZkUsM6Vt.

Burr, M. *Thinking about Linking* (Development Education Association (DEA) Thinkpiece). http://www.dea.org.uk/uploads/4453d22a64a184b4f76a113996448fcf/dea_thinkpiece_ burr.pdf. Accessed 8 July 2008.

Byers, M. 2005. "Are you a global citizen? Really? What does it mean?" *The Tyee*. 5 October 2005. Online at http://thetyee.ca/Views/2005/10/05/globalcitizen/. Archived at http://www.webcitation.org/5XH21lxYr.

Cambridge International Examinations. *IGCSE: Development Studies Syllabus (0453)* (for examination in 2010). http://www.cie.org.uk/qualifications/academic/middlesec/ igcse/subject?assdef_id = 847. Accessed 20 May 2008.

Cambridge International Examinations. *IGCSE: Environmental Management Syllabus (0680)* (for examination in 2010). http://www.cie.org.uk/qualifications/academic/ middlesec/igcse/subject?assdef_id = 855. Accessed 20 May 2008.

Cambridge International Examinations. *Global Perspectives: Pilot Syllabus (0457)* (for examination in 2009). http://www.cie.org.uk/qualifications/ academic/middlesec/igcse/subject?assdef_id = 998. Accessed 20 May 2008.

Cambridge International Examinations. *Pre-U Global Perspectives and the Independent Research Report*. http://www.cie.org.uk/docs/qualifications/preu/syllabus_outlines/ Global%20Perspectives%20and%20Research.pdf. Accessed 20 May 2008.

Cambridge, J. 2003. "Identifying the globalist and internationalist missions of international schools". *International Schools Journal*. Vol XXII, number 2. Pp 54–8.

Cambridge, J. and Carthew, C. 2007. "Schools Self-Evaluating their International Values: A Case Study". In Hayden, M., Levy, J. and Thompson, J. (eds). *The SAGE Handbook of Research in International Education*. London, UK; Thousand Oaks, California; New Delhi, India. Sage Publications. Pp 283–98.

Carlsson-Paige, N. and Lantieri, L. 2005. "A changing vision of education" in Noddings, N. (2005).

Carnegie UK Trust. 2008. *Empowering young people: The final report of the Carnegie Young People's Initiative*. London, UK. Carnegie UK Trust. Online at http:// www.participationworks.org.uk/Portals/0/Files/resources/k-items/carnegie/ empowering%20young%20people%20carnegie.pdf. Accessed 12 April 2008.

Center for Environmental Education and Communications. http://www.chinaeol.net/ en/jypx/jypx_grsch.asp. Accessed 12 November 2007.

Claire, H. and Holden, C. 2007. "The challenge of teaching controversial issues: Principles and practice". In Claire, H. and Holden, C. (eds) *The challenge of teaching controversial issues*. Stoke on Trent, UK and Sterling, Virginia. Trentham Books.

Clark, P. 2000. "A Global Perspective: What does it take?". *Canadian Social Studies*. Vol 35. Online at http://www.quasar.ualberta.ca/css/CSS_35_1/current_concerns_penney_ clark.htm. Archived at http://www.webcitation.org/5XdnBFy0b. Accessed 25 April 2008.

Clarke, P. 2007. "Teaching Controversial Issues in the Classroom—A four-step strategy for clear thinking on controversial issues". *Alberta Teachers Association Magazine*. Vol 87, number 4. Online at http://www.teachers.ab.ca/Quick + Links/Publications/ Magazine/Volume + 87/Number + 4/Articles/Teaching + Controversial + Issues + in + t he + Classroom.htm Archived at http://www.webcitation.org/5XT848jbg. Accessed 30 April 2008.

Clarkeburn, H. 2002. "A test for ethical sensitivity in science". *Journal of Moral Education*. Vol 31. Pp 439–54.

College Board. 2007. *Program Summary Report (2007)*. http://apcentral. collegeboard.com/apc/public/repository/2007_Program_Summary_Report.pdf. Accessed 15 August 2008.

Coumantarakis, S. 1999. *Why Global Education?* Global, Environmental and Outdoor Education Council. http://www.geoec.org/about/why-global.html. Archived at http://www.webcitation.org/5XRazsW8f. Accessed 25 January 2008.

Coumantarakis, S. *Students for Change Action Manual*. Edmonton, Alberta, Canada. University of Alberta, Learning Network. Online at http://www.imminentshift.com/active/activism.pdf. Archived at http://www.webcitation.org/5Y7znNxOg. Accessed 27 May 2008.

Council of Chief State School Officers (CCSSO, USA). 2006. *Global Education: Policy Statement*. Washington, District of Columbia. CCSSO. Online at http://www.ccsso.org/publications/details.cfm?PublicationID = 342. Archived at http://www.webcitation.org/5XISIzAMl.

Council of Europe. 2002. *The Maastricht Global Education Declaration*. http://www.coe.int/t/e/north-south_centre/programmes/3_global_education/b_Maastricht_Declaration/Maastricht_Declaration.pdf. Archived at http://www.webcitation.org/5ZoglnpxR. Accessed 20 February 2008.

Council of International Schools. *The CIS International Student Award*. http://www.cois.org/page.cfm?p = 53. Accessed 30 July 2008.

Curriculum Corporation. 2002. *Global Perspectives: A statement of global education for Australian schools*. Carlton South Victoria, Australia. Curriculum Corporation. Online at http://www.globaleducation.edna.edu.au/globaled/go/engineName/filemanager/pid/122/global_perspectives_statement_2005_web.pdf?actionreq = actionFileDownload&fid = 10828. Archived at http://www.webcitation.org/5YHKKuKti. Accessed 2 June 2008.

Curriculum Corporation. 2005. *Educating for a Sustainable Future: A National Environmental Education Statement for Australian Schools*. http://www.environment.gov.au/education/publications/pubs/sustainable-future.pdf. Accessed 14 March 2008.

Curriculum Corporation. 2007. *Global Perspectives: A statement of global education for Australian schools*. Draft manuscript, 20 November 2007. http://www.curriculum.edu.au/ccsite/cc_global_education,17846.html. Accessed 23 November 2007.

Davies, L. 2002. *Student democracy in England*. http://www.childresearch.net/RESOURCE/RESEARCH/2002/DAVIES.HTM. Accessed 27 March 2008.

Davies, L. 2006. "Global citizenship: Abstraction of framework for action?". *Educational Review*. Vol 58, issue 1. Pp 5–25.

Davies, L. and Kirkpatrick, G. 2000. *The EURIDEM Project: A Review of Student Democracy in Europe*. London, UK. Children's Rights Alliance.

Davies, L., Harber, C. and Yamashita, H. 2004. *Global Citizenship: The Needs of Teachers and Learners*. Birmingham, UK. Centre for International Education and Research. Online at http://www.education.bham.ac.uk/research/cierold/documents/Global_Citizenshop_Report_key_findings.pdf. Archived at http://www.webcitation.org/5XLbtwyQJ. Accessed 15 March 2008.

Davies, L., Williams, C. and Yamashita, H. With Ko Man-Hing, A. 2006. *Inspiring Schools: Impact and Outcomes — Taking up the challenges of pupil participation*. London, UK. Carnegie Young People's Initiative and Esmée Fairbairn Foundation. Online at http://cypi.carnegieuktrust.org.uk/files/InspiringSchools_P1.pdf.

Davies, L. and Yamashita, H. 2007. *School councils — School improvement*. http://www.schoolcouncils.org/resources/research/LSSCARP/. Accessed 2 January 2008.

Davis, J., Ruhe, J., Lee, M. and Rajadhyaksha, U. 2007. "Mission Possible: Do School Mission Statements Work?". *Journal of Business Ethics*. Vol 70, number 1. Pp 99–110.

Deakin Crick, R., Coates, M., Taylor, M. and Ritchie, S. 2004. "A systematic review of the impact of citizenship education on the provision of schooling". *Research Evidence in Education Library*. London, UK. EPPI-Centre, Social Science Research Unit, Institute of Education, University of London. Online at http://eppi.ioe.ac.uk/cms/Default. aspx?tabid = 128. Archived at www.webcitation.org/5XLPCji7P. Accessed 25 April 2008.

Deakin Crick, R., Taylor, M., Tew, M., Samuel, E., Durant, K. and Ritchie, S. 2005. "A systematic review of the impact of citizenship education on student learning and achievement". *Research Evidence in Education Library*. London, UK. EPPI-Centre, Social Science Research Unit, Institute of Education, University of London. Online at http:// eppi.ioe.ac.uk/cms/Default.aspx?tabid = 390. Archived at http://www.webcitation. org/5XLOjso5G. Accessed 25 April 2008.

Dean, B. and Joldoshalieva, R. 2007. "Key strategies for teachers new to controversial issues". In Claire, H. and Holden, C. (eds). *The challenge of teaching controversial issues*. Stoke on Trent, UK and Sterling, Virginia. Trentham Books.

De Caria, P., Garthson, W., Lettieri, J., O'Sullivan, B. and Sicilia, V. 2004. "Infusing Perspectives of Global Citizenship Through School-Wide Initiatives". In Evans, M. and Reynolds, C. (eds). Published online by Ontario Institute for Studies in Education/ University of Toronto at http://cide.oise.utoronto.ca/projects/globalcitizenship/ chap8.pdf. Archived at http://www.webcitation.org/5aR1uS66A. Accessed 28 August 2008.

Department for Education and Skills (DfES). 2005. *Developing the global dimension in the school curriculum*. London, UK. DfES. Online at http://www.teachernet.gov.uk/ publications.

Department for International Development (DFID). 2007. *Partners in Learning: A guide to successful global partnerships*. London, UK. DFID.

Developing Citizenship. *Global days and weeks*. http://www.developingcitizenship.org. uk/curr_global.htm. Accessed 24 June 2008.

Development Education Association (DEA) and Ipsos MORI. 2008. *Our global future: How can education meet the challenge of change? Young people's experiences of global learning*. London, UK. DEA. Online at http://www.dea.org.uk/uploads/4453d22a64a184b4f76a 113996448fcf/Ipsos_MORI.pdf. Archived at http://www.webcitation.org/5ZA0Nz4IH. Accessed 8 July 2008.

Development Education Exchange in Europe Project (DEEEP). http://www.deeep.org.

Dower, N. 2003. *An introduction to global citizenship*. Edinburgh, UK. Edinburgh University Press.

Dower, N. and Williams, J. (eds). 2002. *Global Citizenship: A critical introduction*. New York, New York. Routledge. (Also published by Edinburgh University Press as *Global Citizenship: A critical reader*.)

Downie, R. and Clarkeburn, H. 2005. "Approaches to the Teaching of Bioethics and Professional Ethics in Undergraduate Courses". *Bioscience Education*. Vol 5. Online at http://www.bioscience.heacademy.ac.uk/journal/vol5/Beej-5-2.htm#Clarkeburn02. Archived at www.webcitation.org/5XdhGKo27. Accessed 8 May 2008.

Drake University. *Global Ambassador Program*. http://www.drake.edu/international/cgc/ ambassador.php. Archived at http://www.webcitation.org/5Zh8QdIiz. Accessed 30 July 2008.

East Asia Regional Council of International Schools (EARCOS). http://earcos.org/ std-global.html.

Eco-Schools. http://www.eco-schools.org.

English Secondary Students' Association. *Citizens' juries in schools and colleges.* http://www.studentvoice.co.uk/assets/Citizens'%20Juries%20Toolkit.pdf.

Enviroschools. http://www.enviroschools.org.nz/how_it_works/. Archived at www.webcitation.org/5a2ZbsNsD.

Ethical Corporation. *Child labor in India—A moral red line set in stone.* http://www.ethicalcorp.com/content.asp?ContentID=5332.

European Council of International Schools. *Student award for international understanding.* http://www.ecis.org/student.asp. Accessed 30 July 2008.

Eurydice. 2005. *Citizenship education at school in Europe.* Brussels, Belgium. Eurydice. Online at http://www.eurydice.org/ressources/eurydice/pdf/0_integral/055EN.pdf.

Evans, M. and Reynolds, C. (eds) 2004. *Comparative, International and Development Education Center (CIDEC) Educating for Global Citizenship in a Changing World—A teachers' resource handbook.* Published online by Ontario Institute for Studies in Education, University of Toronto. http://cide.oise.utoronto.ca/globalcitizenship.php.

Fiore, D. J. 2001. *Creating connections for better schools: How leaders enhance school culture.* Larchmont, New York. Eye on Education Inc.

Gearon, L. 2003. *How do we learn to become good citizens?* Southwell, UK. British Educational Research Association.

GLEN (Global Education Network of Young Europeans). http://www.glen-europe.org/index.php?lnk=54. Archived at http://www.webcitation.org/5XRg1H96Q. Accessed 29 April 2008.

Global Citizenship Maturity Test. http://www.peda.net/veraja/jamsa/lukio/oppiaineet/kko/kko1/english. Archived at http://www.webcitation.org/5YdtngR1R. Accessed 15 June 2008.

Global Connections Foundation. http://www.globalconnections.org.

Global Education. http://www.globaleducation.edna.edu.au/.

Global Education Centre. *What is global education?* http://www.globaled.org.nz/about/globaled/. Accessed 23 August 2008.

Global Education Network. 2005. *Guide to Infusing Global Education into the Curriculum.* http://www.global-ed.org/curriculum-guide.pdf. Accessed 10 October 2007.

Global Issues Network. http://www.global-issues-network.org.

Global Leap. http://www.global-leap.org.

GLOBE (Global Learning and Observations to Benefit the Environment). http://www.globe.gov.

Gobar Times Green Schools Programme. http://www.cseindia.org/programme/eeu/html/gobartimesnetwork.asp?id=3.

Goodall, C. 2007. *The Rise and Rise of Climate Care.* http://www.carboncommentary.com/2007/09/15/3#more-3. Archived at http://www.webcitation.org/5Z9lg5ByM. Accessed 8 July 2008.

Green School, Bali. http://www.greenschool.org/.

Greenfield, S. 2008. "'Modern technology is changing the way our brains work,' says neuroscientist". *Daily Mail.* 10 June 2008. Online at http://www.dailymail.co.uk/sciencetech/article-565207/Modern-technology-changing-way-brains-work-says-neuroscientist.html. Archived at http://www.webcitation.org/5YTCiYU6Q.

Gunesch, K. 2007. "International Education's Internationalism: Inspirations from Cosmopolitanism". In Hayden, M. C., Levy, J. and Thompson, J. J. (eds). *Handbook of Research in International Education.* London, UK; Thousand Oaks, California; New Delhi, India. Sage Publications.

Halsey, K., Murfield, J., Harland, J. L., and Lord, P. 2006. *The voice of young people: An engine for improvement? Scoping the evidence.* National Federation for

Educational Research. http://www.cfbt.com/evidenceforeducation/PDF/91151_VoiceOfYoungPeople.pdf.

Hamashita, H. 2006. "Global citizenship education and war: The needs of teachers and learners". *Educational Review*. Vol 58, issue 1. Pp 27–39.

Hanvey, R. G. 1976. *An attainable global perspective*. The American Forum for Global Education. http://www.globaled.org/An_Att_Glob_Persp_04_11_29.pdf.

Hart, R. 1992. *Children's Participation: From tokenism to citizenship*. Florence, Italy. UNICEF Innocenti Research Centre.

Harwood, D. 1997. *Global Express: Tune into the News*. Manchester, UK. Manchester Development Education Project.

Hayden, M. and Thompson, J. 1996. "Potential difference: The driving force for international education". *International Schools Journal*. Vol 16, number 1. Pp 349–61.

Hayden, M. and Thompson, J. 1997. "Student perspectives on international education: A European dimension". *Oxford Review of Education*. Vol 23, number 4. Pp 459–79.

Held, D., McGrew, A., Goldblatt, D. and Perraton, J. (eds). 1999. *Global Transformations*. Cambridge, UK. Polity.

Hertfordshire Grid for Learning. *Good practice case study: The Wroxham School*. http://www.thegrid.org.uk/learning/ict/ks1-2/research/goodpractice/casestudies/thewroxham.shtml. Accessed 15 April 2008.

Hicks, D. 2007a. "Responding to the world". In Hicks, D. and Holden, C. (eds). (2007).

Hicks, D. 2007b. "Principles and precedents". In Hicks, D. and Holden, C. (eds). (2007).

Hicks, D. and Holden, C. (eds) 2007. *Teaching the global dimension: Key principles and effective practice*. London, UK and New York, New York. Routledge.

Hill, I. 2000. "Internationally-minded schools". *International Schools Journal*. Vol XX, number 1. Pp 24–37.

Hill, I. 2007a. "International Education as Developed by the International Baccalaureate Organization". In Hayden, M., Levy, J. and Thompson, J. J. (eds). *Handbook of Research in International Education*. London, UK; Thousand Oaks, California; New Delhi, India. Sage Publications.

Hill, I. 2007b. "Multicultural and International Education: Never the twain shall meet?" *Review of Education*. Vol 53. Pp 245–64.

Hinrichs, J. 2003. "A comparison of levels of international understanding among students of the International Baccalaureate Diploma and Advanced Placement programs in the USA". *Journal of Research in International Education*. Vol 2, number 3. Pp 331–48.

Holden, C. 2007a. "Young people's concerns". In Hicks, D. and Holden, C. (eds). (2007).

Holden, C. 2007b. "Teaching controversial issues". In Hicks, D. and Holden, C. (eds). (2007).

I'Anson, M., Hillier, J., Talbot, J. and Woodhouse, S. 2005. *Global focus weeks in primary schools: A guide for teachers*. Global Dimensions South West, UK. Online at http://www.globaldimensionsouthwest.org.uk/downloads/Global_Focus_Weeks.pdf. Archived at http://www.webcitation.org/5YqPiLVZK. Accessed 24 June 2008.

Inman, S. and Burke, H. 2002. *Schools councils: An apprenticeship in democracy?* http://www.atl.org.uk/atl_en/images/ATL%20Schools%20Councils_tcm2-1691.pdf.

Institute for Global Ethics. *Building Decision Skills*. http://www.globalethics.org/services/edu/bds.htm. Accessed 28 June 2008.

International Association for the Evaluation of Educational Achievements (IEA). *Civic Education Study*. http://www.iea.nl/cived.html. Accessed 15 August 2008.

International Baccalaureate Organization. 1999. *Language A1 guide*. Cardiff, UK. International Baccalaureate Organization.

International Baccalaureate Organization. 2002a. *Language A2 guide*. Cardiff, UK. International Baccalaureate Organization.

International Baccalaureate Organization. 2002b. *Language B guide*. Cardiff, UK. International Baccalaureate Organization.

International Baccalaureate Organization. 2003. *Economics guide*. Cardiff, UK. International Baccalaureate Organization.

International Baccalaureate Organization. 2005. *Programme standards and practices*. Cardiff, UK. International Baccalaureate Organization.

International Baccalaureate Organization. 2006a. *IB learner profile booklet*. Cardiff, UK. International Baccalaureate Organization, and online at http://www.ibo.org/ programmes/documents/learner_profile_en.pdf.

International Baccalaureate Organization. 2006b. *World religions pilot guide*. Cardiff, UK. International Baccalaureate Organization.

International Baccalaureate Organization. 2007a. *Making the PYP happen: A curriculum framework for international primary education*. Cardiff, UK. International Baccalaureate Organization.

International Baccalaureate Organization. 2007b. *Business and management guide*. Cardiff, UK. International Baccalaureate Organization.

International Baccalaureate Organization. 2007c. *The IB Diploma Programme statistical bulletin* (May 2007 session). Cardiff, UK. International Baccalaureate Organization. Online at http://www.ibo.org/facts/statbulletin/documents/ ibdiplomaprogrammemay2007.pdf.

International Baccalaureate Organization. 2008a. *Environmental systems and societies subject outline*. Cardiff, UK. International Baccalaureate Organization.

International Baccalaureate Organization. 2008b. *MYP: From principles into practice*. Cardiff, UK. International Baccalaureate Organization.

International Baccalaureate Organization. 2008c. *Creativity, action, service guide*. Cardiff, UK. International Baccalaureate Organization.

International Education and Resource Network (iEARN). http://www.iearn.org/.

International Networking for Educational Transformation (iNET). http://www.ssat-inet. net/onlineconferences/studentonlineconferences.aspx.

International Primary Curriculum. 2007. http://www.internationalprimarycurriculum. com. Accessed 20 August 2007, 20 May 2008.

InTime. *Evaluating Children's Books for Bias*. http://fp.uni.edu/multiculture/curriculum/ children.htm. Archived at http://www.webcitation.org/5YCk31oOF. Accessed 30 May 2008.

Jerome, L. 2003. *Assessment in Citizenship Education: Workshop booklet*. http://www. citized.info/pdf/commarticles/Lee_Jerome_Assessment_workshop.pdf. Archived at http://www.webcitation.org/5Yfu5ewqx. Accessed 18 June 2008.

Jerome, L., Hayward, J., Easy, J. and Turner, A. N. 2003. *The Citizenship Co-ordinator's Handbook*. Cheltenham, UK. Nelson Thornes.

Johnson, D. W. and Johnson, R. T. 1996. "Conflict resolution and peer mediation programs in elementary and secondary schools: A review of the research". *Review of Educational Research*. Vol 66, number 4. Pp 459–506.

Johnson, K. 2004a. *Children's Voices: Pupil leadership in primary schools*. Slough, UK. National College for School Leadership. Online at http://www.ncsl.org.uk/ media/56F/A3/childrens-voices-summary.pdf. Accessed 18 August 2008.

Johnson, K. 2004b. *Children's Voices: Pupil leadership in primary schools*. Slough, UK. National College for School Leadership. Online at http://www.ncsl.org.uk/ media/56F/B2/childrens-voices.pdf. Accessed 18 August 2008.

Johnston, S., Hughes, G., Bopp, A., Paul, A., Rowlandson, C., Bowers, L., Schumm, G., Manko, L. and Tanner, N. *Students for Change Manual.* University of Alberta, Edmonton, Canada. Learning Network. Online at http://www.imminentshift. com/active/activism.pdf. Archived at http://www.webcitation.org/5aVAvrz1f.

Johnston, W. F. 2008. Personal communication with Boyd Roberts by email, 22 March 2008.

Kaye, C. B. 2003. *The Complete Guide to Service Learning: Proven, Practical Ways to Engage Students in Civic Responsibility, Academic Curriculum, and Social Action.* Minneapolis, Minnesota. Free Spirit Publishing.

Learnscapes. http://www.learnscapes.org/.

Lehigh University. *Global citizenship: A backpack program from Lehigh University.* http:// www.lehigh.edu/~ingc/info.html. Accessed 2 July 2008.

Leming, J. S. 2001. "Integrating a structured ethical reflection curriculum into high school community service experiences: Impact on students' sociomoral development". *Adolescence.* Vol 36. Pp 33–45.

Lewis, C. 2006. "International but not global: How international school curricula fail to address global issues and how this must change". *International Schools Journal.* Vol 25, number 2. Pp 51–67.

Marshall, H. 2005. "Developing The Global Gaze In Citizenship Education: Exploring The Perspectives Of Global Education NGO Workers In England". *International Journal of Citizenship and Teacher Education.* Vol 1, number 2. Pp 76–92. Online at http://www. citized.info/pdf/ejournal/Vol%201%20Number%202/011.pdf. Archived at http:// www.webcitation.org/5ZarSr9tt. Accessed 27 July 2008.

Marshall, H. 2006. "The Global Education Terminology Debate: Exploring some of the issues". In Hayden, M. C., Levy, J. and Thompson, J. J. (eds). *Handbook of Research in International Education.* London, UK; Thousand Oaks, California; New Delhi, India. Sage Publications.

McCreary Centre Society. *Youth Action.* http://www.mcs.bc.ca/ya_ladd.htm. Accessed 15 February 2008.

McKenzie, M. 2004. "More than just a community". *International School.* Vol 7, number 1. Pp 7–9.

McLuhan, M. 1964. *Understanding Media.* New York, New York. Mentor.

Media Awareness Network. http://www.media-awareness.ca.

Mendelovits, J. 2006. *What would an assessment of international mindedness look like? Developing assessments in an unmapped learning area.* Presentation at the Alliance for International Education Conference. Shanghai, China. October 2006.

Merryfield, M. 2004. "The Importance of a Global Education" (Interview with Merry Merryfield by Brian Knighten). *Outreach World.* Online at http://www.outreachworld. org/article.asp?articleid=77. Archived at http://www.webcitation.org/5XdmNJlPV. Accessed 25 April 2008.

Mesa Community College. *Academic Certificate of Global Citizenship.* http://www. mc.maricopa.edu/dept/d10/soc/global/. Accessed 12 August 2008.

Moggach, T. 2006. "Power to the pupil". *Teachers Magazine.* http://www.teachernet.gov. uk/teachers/issue47/primary/features/Powertothepupil/. Archived at http://www. webcitation.org/5a7Ce036T. Accessed 12 April 2008.

Myhill, D. 2007. "Reading the world: Using children's literature to explore controversial issues". In Claire, H. and Holden, C. (eds). *The challenge of teaching controversial issues.* Stoke on Trent, UK and Sterling, Virginia. Trentham Books.

National Association of School Councils (NASC). http://www.nasc.us. Accessed 7 March 2008.

National Service-Learning Clearinghouse. *What is service learning?* http://www. servicelearning.org/what_is_service-learning/service-learning_is/index.php. Accessed 26 July 2008.

National Youth Leadership Council. 2008. *K-12 Service-Learning Standards for Quality Practice.* Saint Paul, Minnesota. NYLC. Online at http://www.nylc.org/objects/ publications/StandardsDoc.pdf. Archived at http://www.webcitation.org/5ZZt7ixVZ. Accessed 25 July 2008.

Noddings, N. (ed). 2005. *Educating citizens for global awareness.* New York, New York. Teachers College Press.

Ord, W. *Assessing citizenship.* http://www.thinkingeducation.co.uk/citedu.htm. Accessed 16 June 2008.

Organisation for Economic Co-operation and Development (OECD). 2005. *Formative Assessment: Improving Learning in Secondary Classrooms.* Paris, France. OECD Publishing. Online at http://www.oecd.org/dataoecd/19/31/35661078.pdf.

Osler, A. and Starkey, H. 2005. *Changing citizenship: Democracy and inclusion in education.* Maidenhead, UK. Open University Press.

Oulton, C., Day, V., Dillon, J., and Grace, M. 2004. "Controversial issues—Teachers' attitudes and practices in the context of citizenship education". *Oxford Review of Education.* Vol 30, number 4. Pp 489–507.

Oxfam. 2006a. *Education for Global Citizenship—A guide for schools.* Oxford, UK. Oxfam GB. Online at http://www.oxfam.org.uk/coolplanet/teachers/globciti/downloads/ gccurriculum.pdf. Archived at http://www.webcitation.org/5XISkdFvQ.

Oxfam. 2006b. *Teaching controversial issues.* Oxford, UK. Oxfam GB and online at http:// www.oxfam.org.uk/education.

Oxfam. 2007. *Building successful school partnerships.* Oxford, UK. Oxfam GB. Online at http://www.oxfam.org.uk/education/teachersupport/cpd/partnerships/files/oxfam_ gc_guide_building_successful_school_partnerships.pdf.

Oxfam. 2008. *Before you start raising money ... an Oxfam guide for schools.* Oxford, UK. Oxfam GB.

Pandit, K. and Alderman, D. 2004. "Border crossings in the classroom: The international student interview as a strategy for promoting international understanding". *Journal of Geography.* Vol 103. Pp 127–36.

Parker, W. C., Ninomiya, A. and Cogan, J. 1999. "Educating World Citizens: Towards Multinational Curriculum Development". *American Educational Research Journal.* Vol 36, number 2. Pp 117–45.

Parra Youth Matters. 2003. *Media, culture and youth: Recommendations from the Youth Jury.* http://www.activedemocracy.net/parrayouth/parra_youth_matters_report.pdf.

Peer Resources. *Peer Helping Brochure and National Standards.* http://www.peer.ca/broch. html. Accessed 27 March 2008.

Pettigrew, T. F. and Tropp, L. R. 2000. "Does intergroup contact reduce prejudice? Recent meta-analytic findings". In Oscamp, S. (ed). *Reducing prejudice and discrimination.* Mahwah, New Jersey. Erlbaumthrough.

Pike, G. and Selby, D. 1988. *Global Teacher, Global Learner.* London, UK. Hodder and Stoughton.

Pike, G. and Selby, D. 1999. *In the Global Classroom 1.* Toronto, Canada. Pippin Publishing.

Pike, G. and Selby, D. 2000. *In the Global Classroom 2.* Toronto, Canada. Pippin Publishing.

Potter, J. 2002. *Active citizenship in schools.* London, UK and Sterling, Virginia. Kogan Page.

Price, J. 2003. *Get Global: A skill-based approach to active global citizenship.* Action Aid, UK. Online at http://www.getglobal.org.uk/.

Qualifications and Curriculum Authority (QCA). 2006. *Assessing citizenship. Example assessment activities for key stage 3.* London, UK. Qualifications and Curriculum Authority. Online at http://www.qca.org.uk.

Reed, J. and Koliba, C. 1995. *Facilitating Reflection: A Manual for Leaders and Educators.* http://www.uvm.edu/~dewey/reflection_manual/. Accessed 18 June 2008.

Ribble, M. *Nine Themes of Digital Citizenship.* http://www.digitalcitizenship.net/Nine_Elements.html. Archived at http://www.webcitation.org/5Z8RnSdBB. Accessed 7 July 2008.

Ribble, M. and Bailey, G. 2007. *Digital citizenship in schools.* Eugene, Oregon. ISTE (International Society for Technology in Education).

Ribble, M. and Bailey, G. *Teaching Digital Citizenship Reflection: A Four-Stage Technology Learning Framework.* http://coe.ksu.edu/digitalcitizenship/DCReflect.pdf. Archived at http://www.webcitation.org/5Z8PWsLx5. Accessed 7 July 2008.

Rischard, J. F. 2008. In a lecture at the Global Issues Network conference. Beijing, China. April 2008. Also expressed in various lectures in 2007.

Roberts, B. 2002. *What should international education be? From emergent theory to practice.* Paper presented at the Alliance for International Education conference. Geneva, Switzerland. September 2002.

Roberts, B. 2003. "What should international education be? From emergent theory to practice". *International Schools Journal.* Vol XXII, number 2. Pp 69–79.

Roberts, B. 2006. *Not so much a subject, more a way of life.* Presentation at the Alliance for International Education conference. Shanghai, China. October 2006.

Roberts, B. 2007. "Making global citizenship international—A call for concerted action". *International School.* Vol 9, number 2. Pp 15–16.

Roberts, B. 2008. "The IGC Award takes off". *International School.* Vol 10, number 2. Pp 9–10.

Rogers, M. 1998. "Student responses to learning about futures". In Hicks, D. and Slaughter, R. (eds). *Futures Education: World Yearbook of Education.* London. Kogan Page.

Roots and Shoots. http://www.rootsandshoots.org/. Accessed 10 February 2008.

Round Square. http://www.roundsquare.org/. Accessed 11 August 2008.

Rudduck, J. 2006. "The past, the papers and the project". *Educational Review.* Vol 58, number 2. Pp 131–43.

Save the Children UK and the Scottish Alliance for Children's Rights. 2007. *The recruitment pack: Involving children & young people in the recruitment of staff.* Edinburgh, UK. Save the Children and the Scottish Alliance for Children's Rights.

Schaffer, R. H. and Thomson, H. A. 1992. "Successful change programs begin with results". *Harvard Business Review.* January–February 1992.

Schattle, H. 2008. *The Practices of Global Citizenship.* Lanham, Maryland. Rowman and Littlefield.

Schein, E. 1992. *Organizational Culture and Leadership* (2nd edition). San Francisco, California. Jossey-Bass.

Scholte, J. A. 2002. *What Is Globalization? The Definitional Issue—Again.* CSGR Working Paper. Number 109/02. Centre for the Study of Globalisation and Regionalisation. University of Warwick, UK. http://www2.warwick.ac.uk/fac/soc/csgr/research/workingpapers/2002/wp10902.pdf.

School Councils UK. http://www.schoolcouncils.org. Accessed 12 February 2008.

Schweisfurth, M. 2006. "Education for global citizenship: Teacher agency and curricular structure in Ontario schools". *Educational Review*. Vol 58, number 1. Pp 41–50. Online at http://www.healthpromotingschools.co.uk/practitioners/schoolethos/index.asp.

Selfridge, J. 2004. "The Resolving Conflict Creatively Program: How we know it works". *Theory into Practice*. Vol 43, number 1. Pp 59–67.

Simandiraki, A. and Yao, Z. 2004. *Developing an instrument to evaluate students' internationally minded values*. Presentation at the Alliance for International Education conference. Düsseldorf, Germany. October 2004.

Skidmore, D. 2002. "From pedagogical dialogue to dialogic pedagogy". *Language and Education*. Vol 14, number 4. Pp 283–96.

Snowball, L. 2007. "Becoming more internationally-minded: International teacher certification and professional development". In Hayden, M., Levy, J., and Thompson, J. (eds). *The SAGE Handbook of Research in International Education*. London, UK; Thousand Oaks, California; New Delhi, India. Sage Publications.

Stevahn, L. 2004. "Integrating conflict resolution into the curriculum". *Theory into Practice*. Vol 43, number 1. Pp 50–58.

Sustainable Schools. http://www.teachernet.gov.uk/sustainableschools/. Accessed 12 August 2008.

Sutcliffe, D. 2006. "International education and conflict". *International Schools Journal* . Vol 25, number 2. Pp 80–85.

Symes, B. 1995. *Marshall McLuhan's "Global Village"*. http//www.aber.ac.uk/media/Students/bas9401.html. Archived at http://www.webcitation.org/5ZoaGYiWX. Accessed 3 January 2008.

Sweet, M. E. 2007. "Review of Osler, Audrey & Starkey, Hugh (2005). *Changing citizenship: Democracy and inclusion in education*". In *Education Review* (October 2007). Online at http://edrev.asu.edu/reviews/rev600.htm. Archived at http://www.webcitation.org/5XH5wYPsn.

Thompson, J. 1998. "Towards a model for international education". In Hayden, M. and Thompson, J. (eds). *International Education: Principles and practice*. London, UK and Sterling, Virginia. Kogan Page.

Thornton, S. 2005. "Incorporating Internationalism into the Social Studies Curriculum". In Noddings, N. (ed). *Educating citizens for global awareness*. New York, New York. Teachers College Press.

Through Other Eyes. http://www.throughothereyes.org.uk.

Tye, K. A. 1999. "Global education: A worldwide movement". *Issues in Global Education*. Number 150. Online at http://www.globaled.org/issues/150. Accessed 4 February 2008.

UKOWLA (UK One World Linking Association). 2006. *Toolkit for Linking: Opportunities and challenges*. Somerset, UK. UKOLA. Online at http://www.ukowla.org.uk/main/toolkit.asp.

University of British Columbia. *Perspectives on Global Citizenship Syllabus 2008–2009*. http://olt.ubc.ca/SOCI430_Syllabus.pdf.

Urry, J. 1999. "Globalisation and Citizenship". *Journal of World System Research*. Vol 2. Pp 311–324.

US Partnership for Education for Sustainable Development. 2008. *National Education for Sustainability K–12 Student Learning Standards*. http://www.uspartnership.org.

US Scouting Service Project. 2006. *Citizenship in the World*. http://meritbadge.org/wiki/index.php/Citizenship_in_the_World. Accessed 15 August 2008.

Van Oord, L. 2006. "Peace and Conflict Studies: The first three decades". *International Schools Journal*. Vol 25, number 2. Pp 8–13.

Van Oord, L. 2008. "Peace Education: An International Baccalaureate perspective". *Journal of Peace Education*. Vol 5, number 1. Pp 49–62.

Victoria International Development Education Association. http://www.videa.ca/global/citizen.html. Accessed 1 February 2008.

Viroqua Elementary and Liberty Pole Center Parent–Student Handbook. 2001. http://www2.dpi.state.wi.us/sig/assessment/soh/examples/WINNS_missionstatement_viroqua.PDF. Archived at http://www.webcitation.org/5YfhLbPl2. Accessed 18 June 2008.

Walker, G. 2006. *Educating the Global Citizen*. Saxmundham, UK. John Catt Educational Ltd.

Walker, G. 2007. Conferences—"Affair[s] of masks and mystification". George Walker's weblog. http://blogs.ibo.org/georgew/2007/11/24/. Archived at http://www.webcitation.org/5YuMKo7Pu. Accessed 24 November 2007.

Weaver, G. (ed). 2000. *Culture, Communication and Conflict* (2nd edition). Boston, Massachusetts. Pearson Publishing.

Wei, B. 2003. "Being a successful global citizen is important". *Spartan Daily*. 13 November 2003. Online at http://www.engr.sjsu.edu/media/pdf/dean/speech/spartan_daily_global_citizen_111303.pdf. Archived at http://www.webcitation.org/5XFZAEYzP. Accessed 20 June 2006.

What Works Clearinghouse. 2006. *Intervention: Building Decision Skills*. http://ies.ed.gov/ncee/wwc/reports/character_education/bds/. Accessed 28 June 2008.

Whitty, G. and Wisby, E. 2007. Real *Decision Making? School Councils in Action*. London. Department for Children, Schools and Families. Online at http://www.dfes.gov.uk/research/data/uploadfiles/DCSF-RR001.pdf.

World Commission on the Environment and Development. 1987. *Report of the World Commission on Environment and Development: Our Common Future (The Brundtland Report)*. http://www.un-documents.net/wced-ocf.htm. Accessed 15 February 2008.

Worldmapper. http://www.worldmapper.org.

Worldwide Fund for Nature (WWF). 2008. *2010 and beyond: Rising to the biodiversity challenge*. Gland, Switzerland. WWF. Online at http://www.zsl.org/science/news/biodiversity-plummeting,458,NS.html.

Worldwide Fund for Nature (WWF). *Pathways: A developmental framework for school sustainability*. http://www.wwflearning.org.uk/data/files/pathways-310.pdf.

Young, M. and Commins, E. 2002. *Global Citizenship: The Handbook for Primary Teaching*. Oxford, UK: Oxfam GB. Cambridge, UK: Chris Kington Publishing.

Appendix: IB learner profile

The aim of all IB programmes is to develop internationally minded people who, recognizing their common humanity and shared guardianship of the planet, help to create a better and more peaceful world.

IB learners strive to be:

Inquirers
They develop their natural curiosity. They acquire the skills necessary to conduct inquiry and research and show independence in learning. They actively enjoy learning and this love of learning will be sustained throughout their lives.

Knowledgeable
They explore concepts, ideas and issues that have local and global significance. In so doing, they acquire in-depth knowledge and develop understanding across a broad and balanced range of disciplines.

Thinkers
They exercise initiative in applying thinking skills critically and creatively to recognize and approach complex problems, and make reasoned, ethical decisions.

Communicators
They understand and express ideas and information confidently and creatively in more than one language and in a variety of modes of communication. They work effectively and willingly in collaboration with others.

Principled
They act with integrity and honesty, with a strong sense of fairness, justice and respect for the dignity of the individual, groups and communities. They take responsibility for their own actions and the consequences that accompany them.

Open-minded
They understand and appreciate their own cultures and personal histories, and are open to the perspectives, values and traditions of other individuals and communities. They are accustomed to seeking and evaluating a range of points of view, and are willing to grow from the experience.

Caring
They show empathy, compassion and respect towards the needs and feelings of others. They have a personal commitment to service, and act to make a positive difference to the lives of others and to the environment.

Risk-takers	They approach unfamiliar situations and uncertainty with courage and forethought, and have the independence of spirit to explore new roles, ideas and strategies. They are brave and articulate in defending their beliefs.
Balanced	They understand the importance of intellectual, physical and emotional balance to achieve personal well-being for themselves and others.
Reflective	They give thoughtful consideration to their own learning and experience. They are able to assess and understand their strengths and limitations in order to support their learning and personal development.

Index

NOTE: Page numbers in *italic* refer to tables and figures.